YOGA THERAPY

SAFE, NATURAL METHODS TO PROMOTE HEALING AND RESTORE HEALTH AND WELL-BEING

Stella Weller

Thorsons
An Imprint of HarperCollins*Publishers*

Thorsons
An Imprint of HarperCollins*Publishers*
77–85 Fulham Palace Road
Hammersmith, London W6 8JB

Published by Thorsons 1995
5 7 9 10 8 6

A catalogue record for this book
is available from the British Library

ISBN 0 7225 2998 8

Typeset by Harper Phototypesetters Limited,
Northampton, England.
Printed in Great Britain by Scotprint Ltd, Musselburgh

CONTENTS

ACKNOWLEDGEMENTS

Many thanks to everyone who helped me prepare this book, especially John Hardaker and Erica Smith, Lisa Eaton, and the design team at Thorsons. I am particularly grateful to my husband, Walter, for his steadfastness and encouragement.

INTRODUCTION

The awareness that we should take greater responsibility for our own health and wellbeing, rather than rely on treatments that merely mask or suppress symptoms of health disorders, continues to grow. The already enlightened know of the intimate relationship that exists between body and mind, and realize that they have within them vast, largely untapped, natural resources without which no treatment administered by an outside agent (the healer without) can be fully effective. These inner resources (the healer within) can be mobilized in various ways including self-awareness, self-discipline and self-help, all of which are essential components of a superb, ancient and highly respected health system called *yoga*.

Coming from the Sanskrit word *yuj*, which means to join or integrate, yoga is an approach to health which aims to help all your body's components work together in harmony. Because yoga has its roots in the Hindu culture of India, there is a popular misconception that it is a religion. This is not at all the case. Yoga is non-sectarian and may be practised with confidence by anyone. There is absolutely nothing magical or occult about yoga.

The most popular form of yoga, increasingly practised in the Western world, is *Hatha Yoga*, or 'the yoga of health'. This is used in many health-promotion programmes as a basic framework, because it is an effective way to reduce stress. Its primary goal is to prevent illness or, if illness already exists, to help regain and maintain optimum health. It achieves this through a balanced regime of bodily and mental training. The physical exercises (*asanas* or postures) benefit not only muscles and joints, but also internal organs, nerves and glands. In addition to this, the practice of yoga prevents tension build-up and trains and disciplines your mind in a way that improves concentration, and therefore productivity. Yoga's mental and breathing exercises are perhaps unsurpassed for combating stress. Through regular practice you learn to acquire a sense of your integrated – whole – self.

Because of this focused approach to exercise, yoga gives you a keener sense of body awareness, which alerts you to the earliest symptoms and signs of departure from good health. This training has far-reaching benefits in that it helps you to cope more positively with life's ups and downs. You learn to care for yourself in every aspect of your life.

Part 1 of this book deals with what yoga is and is not; what it embraces and how it heals. It is an inspirational section that encourages you to try yoga to help prevent health disorders, and to incorporate it into your daily life to attain and maintain the best possible health. You will read about those who have used yoga techniques to help them stop smoking, prevent major back problems, overcome the sometimes distressing symptoms of menopause, lose weight and maintain weight loss, deal constructively with anxiety, manage stress better, and so on. This section also includes a chapter on healing nutrients.

Part 2 describes the yoga exercises: preparing for them; warming-up and cooling-down; and the postures (*asanas*), which are divided into sitting, standing, forwards bending, backwards bending, lateral bending and twisting, lying, inverted and 'series' exercises. This section also deals with breathing, concentration and relaxation exercises. There are some additional exercises for the eyes and hands, as well as special hygienic practices. Clear line drawings illustrate the exercises, and, where appropriate, cautions are given for the practice of the exercises.

Part 3 is, in effect, a lexicon of about 100 common disorders. These include: anxiety, arthritis, back problems, balding, colds, fatigue, insomnia, panic attacks, premenstrual syndrome, stress and varicose veins. Brief notes are given on each condition, and referral is made to the pertinent exercise(s) in Part 2, and to specific beneficial nutrients.

Yoga Therapy offers an opportunity to explore and refine those processes that help mobilize your healer within to complement the care provided by your healer without – your doctor or other therapist. Do not, however, expect immediate, dramatic results. The benefits you gain from practising the techniques in this book will be proportionate to the consistency of your practice. If you are faithful, you can look forward to accumulating benefits which will manifest themselves in improved health and vitality. If disease does strike, you will have greater resources to combat it than if you had not made the yoga programme a part of your daily routine. Although no cures are promised, diligent practice of the exercises will help create favourable conditions for your body's own healing forces to bring about remission or healing.

Yoga Therapy is for everyone. It may be used as a workbook and handy reference for those who prefer to practise in the privacy of their own homes. It may also be used as a resource for fitness instructors and health professionals, such as doctors, nurses, physiotherapists and community health workers.

The suggestions and techniques outlined in this book are intended as a supplement to proper medical attention and not as a substitute for it. For optimum results, I encourage you to combine the best that orthodox medicine has to offer with yoga and/or other appropriate complementary therapy.

PART ONE

YOGA: WHAT IT IS AND HOW IT HEALS

CHAPTER ONE

WHAT IS YOGA?

Yoga means integration or wholeness. The yogic concept of the working of the body and mind is that there is, in both, a homoeostatic mechanism which contributes to balanced, integrating functioning, and that each person has an inherent power of adaptation. (Homoeostasis refers to the maintenance of steady states.) Yoga considers the human being as a *whole* and does not divide you into watertight compartments. It provides ways and means of helping your body and mind to maintain a state of balance, or to regain it quickly if it is disturbed.

You may wish to think of yoga as a useful package containing effective stress-reduction practices such as gentle stretching, breathing, meditation and relaxation exercises. If you are uncomfortable with the word *yoga*, simply think of it as a superb approach to healthy, harmonious living. Consider also that many westerners practise Japanese martial arts without becoming Buddhists!

Hatha Yoga consists of non-strenuous physical exercises which take each joint in the body through its full range of motion, strengthening, stretching gently and balancing each part. The practice of these exercises requires a complete focusing on what is being done, so that it is virtually impossible to hurt yourself. The exercises are performed in synchronization with regular breathing to provide oxygen to the working muscles. They affect not only joints and muscles, but also organs, glands and other body structures. The exercises also teach you to work within your limits in a non-judgemental way.

The breathing exercises, collectively known as *pranayama*, as well as the concentration, meditation and relaxation techniques, are extremely effective in diverting attention from disturbing environmental stimuli and so help you become more focused. This brings a feeling of greater self-control; a feeling that you are less at the mercy of outside influences. Practising these techniques also helps you to conserve energy and to manage pain and other forms of stress more effectively.

Yoga differs from other types of exercises in that it engages the *whole* person. Because it requires awareness during practice, mind and body work together to create physiological and psychological (body—mind) harmony, which in turns leads to optimum potential for healing.

Yoga is not a quick fix, though, so do not expect dramatic results as soon as you start practising it. Just as the steady drip of water eventually reshapes a stone, the regular practice of yoga exercises heals and restructures damaged body tissues in a slow and steady way. At the same time, it will help you to recover from the psychological effects of pain and disability.

Doctors can limit the damage caused by disease-producing germs through the use of specific drugs, and surgeons can stitch a wound or reset a broken bone – but the actual healing comes from within. It is the body that mobilizes its biological energies to stimulate tissues to proliferate (increase self-reproduction) and seal a wound or weld a fractured bone.

Regular yoga practice trains your system to conserve energy, and to reorganize and revitalize itself in a way that enables it to function more effectively. It will create favourable conditions for inherent healing forces to operate advantageously. So, when disease does strike, your body will have ample resources to deal with it. Yoga therapy, in essence, is both preventive and curative. Daily practice can help restore your natural balance and harmony, and bring health to every aspect of your life.

CHAPTER TWO

HOW YOGA HEALS

Yogic practices aim at developing and strengthening immunity to those influences, from within and without, that might contribute to any sort of disintegration. They achieve this by bringing about an altered adaptability of the tissues forming the various organs and systems of the body. Yoga exercises, in short, recondition mind and body.

Yoga has an integrated approach to attaining and maintaining good health. You can therefore expect better results from regular yoga practice than you can from any system that places emphasis only on the signs and symptoms of disease, rather than on the less evident, but very important, underlying causes.

Yoga's stretching, strengthening and meditative exercises are effective because they encourage full focusing on the movements and the body parts involved. Used as a door into your body-mind awareness, yoga can teach you many useful lessons for practical application to everyday living: how to conserve rather than squander energy; how to be alert to early symptoms of any departure from good health; how to detect habitual faulty postures and movements that may, in time, compromise optimum functioning; what your physical limitations are and how best to work with them.

Through practising yoga you come to know your body on a totally intimate level. This moment-to-moment mindfulness is excellent for promoting calm and control – invaluable attributes for proofing yourself against the stresses of life. Yoga trains mind and body to work together to create a healing environment.

About a week before writing the above, I met a woman (I shall call her Laurie) whom I had not seen for about 15 years. She remembered me as her yoga instructor, and began to reminisce about the good times she had had in our classes. She had nothing but praise for yoga which, she said, had made a significant difference to the quality of her life.

Laurie's problems had been threefold: high blood pressure; having a child who was perceived as abnormal by her peers and who was the target of cruel jokes; and an impatient, volatile husband who handled stress poorly. A friend diagnosed with MS (multiple sclerosis) had encouraged Laurie to join a yoga class at a local community centre, and it was there that I first met her.

Today, Laurie's blood pressure is within normal range, and she maintains this with faithful practice of a superb relaxation technique called the Pose of Tranquility (*see Chapter 6, page 51*). Because of the well-known benefits of this exercise in helping to reduce high blood pressure, Laurie was able to persuade her doctor (who was receptive to yoga) to halve, then later further reduce, her medication dosage.

Laurie told me that the breathing techniques she had learned in our classes had proved indispensable during the countless times she had had to battle with the anger and frustration inherent in protecting her child from the insults of her classmates. The practice of these techniques had helped her maintain control and dignity which, she believes, were instrumental in preventing her daughter from coming to any physical harm. They were a boon, as well, in helping her exercise patience in dealing with her husband's not infrequent outbursts. All in all, said Laurie, the yoga techniques she practised, and continues to practise, have helped her acquire needed strength.

Now in her late 40s, Laurie is using yoga for yet another reason. She is experiencing the hot flushes not uncommon to women approaching or going through menopause. Yoga, she stated, helps her manage her menopausal symptoms with an equanimity that was unknown to her 16 years ago.

I watched Laurie and her husband talk to and tease each other on the boat on which we were all passengers. I had the impression that she, her husband and her daughter (now 22 and still living at home) had all managed to overcome serious difficulties and emerge intact and with joy. I do believe that yoga has played no small part in the quality of their lives, and feel privileged to have been able to show Laurie how to use tools she already owned to handle skilfully some of life's adversities.

THE THREE-STEP APPROACH TO HEALTH

Three integral steps are employed in the yogic approach to restoring and maintaining optimum health:

1. Cultivating correct psychological attitudes through mental exercises and breathing and relaxation techniques.
2. Reconditioning nerve-muscle and nerve-gland systems (the whole body, in effect) to enable them to withstand high levels of stress and strain. This is achieved through physical and breathing exercises.
3. Encouraging the intake of a health-promoting diet and the natural elimination of wastes.

BREATHING AND RELAXATION

The breathing exercises, apart from bringing a richer oxygen supply to all tissues, train you to shift your attention away from disturbing stimuli and to focus instead on breathing processes. This has a calming effect on your entire system and helps you to acquire or recapture a sense of control and self-reliance. You begin to realize that you are no longer totally at the mercy of outside influences, and that you do have inner strengths on which you can rely. Practised regularly in conjunction with the relaxation techniques, yoga breathing exercises help to release you from slavery to states such as anxiety, and from cravings for and dependency on health-destroying substances such as nicotine. This is what Edwin discovered.

I met Edwin about 25 years ago. He was then 30 years old and a cigarette smoker. Smoking cigarettes however, was not in his best interests, particularly since he needed to preserve a healthy respiratory system (he was a promising tenor).

Edwin's singing teacher gave him certain exercises to do. They were very reminiscent of yoga breathing and relaxation exercises. As Edwin practised them faithfully, I noticed that he smoked less and less, until one day he stopped smoking altogether. I remarked on this.

Edwin then told me that he actually used to enjoy smoking and did not particularly set out to give it up, although he knew how detrimental it was to his voice and health. '*I* didn't give it up,' he said, '*it* gave me up.' He had noticed, he explained, that as he persevered with the breathing exercises he felt less and less tense and anxious, and did not seem to crave cigarettes the way he used to. In time, he lost all interest in them and, as his lifestyle improved in general, he has never resumed smoking.

Edwin has not touched a cigarette in two decades! Moreover, the stomach ulcer that once plagued him has healed and has never returned – without medical or surgical intervention. He conceded that the breathing and relaxation techniques, along with a more wholesome diet and the fact that he now expresses himself more readily rather than keeping things bottled up inside, have all combined to make him the healthiest he has ever been.

Regularly practised yoga breathing exercises have other health advantages. That is why, increasingly, they are being incorporated into health-promotion programmes of all kinds. They are a handy tool for relieving the distress inherent in breathing disorders such as asthma.

About a year before I started writing this book, I talked with Joan, a nursing instructor, who suffers from this condition. She described to me her feelings of being close to death in the summer of that year when she was on holiday with her husband. She had been prescribed a medication from the NSAID (non-steroidal anti-inflammatory drugs) family for the arthritis she suffered in her hands, feet and hips. But this particular drug was contraindicated for people with asthma, and neither Joan nor her doctor (surprisingly) was aware of this. The drug precipitated a severe asthma attack and Joan had to be rushed to the casualty department of the nearest hospital. 'That was the closest I've come to meeting my Maker,' Joan told me as she related these events.

Now Joan is back teaching nursing once again, the offending medication having been discontinued. She attends a respiratory rehabilitation clinic where she is taught breathing and relaxation exercises, among them the Whispering Breath which is described in Chapter 7. Joan, who is now in her 50s, says that she has never felt better.

PHYSICAL EXERCISES (*ASANAS*)

Yoga exercises (*asanas* or postures) are possibly the best tools for disrupting learned patterns of wrong muscular efforts, and re-establishing harmonious functioning of the whole system. Because many people in industrialized societies spend a great deal of time sitting – at work, in a car and in front of a television set – the body begins to atrophy (waste away) through disuse. Joints become stiff and muscles become flabby.

For those who have not really used their body for years, yoga exercises are a wonderful, gentle way to bring about beneficial change. They can reverse disuse atrophy because they incorporate a full-body musculoskeletal (pertaining to the muscles and skeleton) conditioning and strengthening exercises. Moreover, because the exercises are performed mindfully – that is, with full awareness of what is being done – they are excellent for counteracting the 'scattered' thinking characteristic of anxiety states, and for promoting calm and control. The synchronized breathing required for the proper execution of yoga exercises, and therefore for their effectiveness, further enhances this feeling of quiet self-assuredness as built-up tension is released, and a sense of being in touch with yourself, at a deep level, becomes apparent.

Perhaps no one I have met can better attest to these facts than Kay. I met her when she was an overweight young mother. During the week, her husband was away at work all day. There was little companionship for her other than that provided by her two children, both under five years old. The family lived in a remote, isolated community where the nearest neighbour was miles away.

Kay, a qualified teacher who had decided that she would stay at home once a child was born, found herself turning to food for solace, trying to fill a certain emptiness she felt but which would not be satisfied. As she gained weight she lost self-esteem and confidence, and soon became very depressed.

Then one day a book arrived in the post. It was a yoga book sent to her by her aunt, who had been experiencing unpleasant menopausal symptoms. Her accompanying letter described the marvellous transformation she was undergoing through diligent practice of yoga exercises. The hot flushes and depression she had been experiencing had all but disappeared since attending yoga classes at a local community school. 'You must give it a try, Kay,' her aunt urged her in the letter.

And so Kay, at first sceptically, attempted the simple yoga postures and breathing exercises, as well as the Pose of Tranquility (*see page 51*) which she did each evening when the children were in bed. She credits

her teacher's training with the discipline that permitted her to stick with the exercises and not give up simply because noticeable results were neither immediate nor dramatic. In addition, she corresponded with her aunt more often than she had done previously, and a mutual support system came into being.

Then Kay's husband was transferred to another town, not as isolated as the one in which they lived. Kay was now able to attend yoga classes once a week at a centre not far from their home, while her husband looked after the children.

Not a year later, Kay was almost unrecognizable: she had turned from an obese, depressed housewife into a trim, energetic, cheerful individual to whom people were attracted. Soon afterwards, she was asked to teach the yoga classes when the regular instructor moved to another town. Kay has never looked back, and she has nothing but praise for yoga which, she told me, brought her back to life. Indeed, today Kay actively participates in her community where she is a valued and respected member.

There are many others who have high praise for the yoga health system. I am still in touch with one of them, a woman called Dorrie. She was a student in a yoga class which I was asked to establish and instruct years ago, specifically for people with MS (multiple sclerosis).

Dorrie, an attractive, petite, young-looking 40-year-old, worked as a hostess at a local golf club, a job requiring much energy and many hours on her feet. She had been referred to my class because she was beginning to tire more easily than before, and also to feel some loss of strength in her legs. Understandably, she was also starting to experience increased anxiety.

As a yoga student, Dorrie worked conscientiously at her exercises, responding well to encouragement to try again when she could not maintain the steadiness demanded by the balancing postures. I remember her, on one occasion, sharply reprimanding another student who was habitually whining 'I'll never be able to do that.' (To her own surprise, the student *did* eventually execute the posture in question.)

Today, more than 10 years later, Dorrie's condition has not worsened as predicted by certain doctors. She no longer works at the golf club, but she walks and incorporates various yoga techniques into her daily activities of farm work and housework. The anti-anxiety medication she regularly took when I first met her has been reduced to a very small dose, to be taken only when absolutely necessary. Dorrie tells me that this is not often. When she feels anxiety coming on, she practises the Anti-Anxiety Breath described in Chapter 7. She says she finds it very effective, bringing relief in as little as two minutes of practice. When I last spoke to Dorrie she sounded cheerful and fulfilled. 'I'm not in a wheelchair yet,' she assured me.

CHARACTERISTICS COMMON TO THE EXERCISES

1. Each yoga exercise (*asana* or posture) involves a contraction of some muscle groups and the relaxation of their antagonists (those which counteract the action of the contracted muscles). By consciously pitting various groups of muscles against their antagonists, each exercise first brings an awareness of faulty postural habits, then helps correct them, as well as encouraging conservation of energy.

2. When assuming a given position, you visualize (usually with eyes closed) energy flowing into the muscles, bringing health and healing. The full attention given to what you are doing facilitates the process. In time, with faithful practice, this visualization becomes an awareness of internal organs and other structures that lie under the muscles. You may experience this as a pleasant warmth in the appropriate part of the body. Long after the exercise is over, muscular relaxation persists in the form of a 'visceral silence' – a quieting of internal organs, particularly those within the abdomen. By repeating the exercises daily, you learn to bring your body to a standstill, with the spine in good alignment. This is essential for calming nervous activity, and for the reduction of wear and tear on the entire system.

3. Each exercise brings into action all the muscles and joints of a given body part. With regular practice, muscles that tend to waste away through lack of use, such as the abdominal muscles, receive a better blood supply and begin to function more efficiently. Muscles and joints that feel somewhat sore and resisting at first, soon become freely movable. They also become less vulnerable to injury and disease.

4. Each exercise involves the vertebral column (spine), subjecting it to gentle tractions (pulling) and/or torsions (rotations) of varying degrees. This promotes an awareness of good postural habits and body mechanics, which are so vital to the health of the spine and related structures. I can personally vouch for all this.

When I was 16 years old, a doctor discovered that I had a scoliosis (a lateral spinal curvature). In those days there was neither the technology nor the money to correct the condition, and I had to learn to live with it as best I could.

Today, decades later, I work 12-hour shifts in a hospital, look after a family of four and write books. My scoliosis is still marked, but I hardly ever feel pain and I am seldom ill enough to absent myself from work. I attribute my health and productivity largely to the yoga principles of exercise and relaxation, to which I have faithfully adhered.

You can learn more about yoga for back care in my book entitled *The Yoga Back Book* (*see Bibliography for details*).

5. Some exercises seem to require a great deal of effort. As yoga training progresses, this effort is gradually eliminated. The regular practitioner is able to achieve and maintain positions of balance with economical expenditure of energy. This ability to retain equilibrium with little effort has important psychological implications: the regular yoga practitioner is able to maintain calm and control in stressful situations, and to act appropriately rather than react inappropriately.

WHAT TO EXPECT

What can you expect from incorporating yoga exercises – mental and physical – into your daily schedule? What can you expect from 15 to 20 minutes of diligent practice morning and evening, or about half-an-hour once a day?

You can expect your joints to lose their stiffness and become more freely movable. You can expect better muscle tone. You can, in short, expect a more flexible body and fewer aches and pains. You can look forward to having the self-control and self-confidence to deal more effectively with emotions such as frustration and anger, and with states such as an anxiety and depression.

With adherence to a health-promoting diet and a greater awareness of the dangers of becoming overweight, your body will become firmer and lighter and your heart will pump blood more efficiently through blood vessels that are more elastic and less clogged with impurities. Other major organs will benefit from the practice of the breathing exercises, which also strengthen the respiratory and nervous systems. Your entire body will be reorganized and revitalized, and it will function more economically.

Practising meditation and the all-body relaxation technique (*see Pose of Tranquility, page 51*) daily will help to quieten any restlessness of the mind. It will help the conscious mind relax while maintaining awareness; a state doctors refer to as 'restful alertness'. Among many other benefits, a period of daily meditation will help keep blood pressure within normal limits, and discourage stomach and intestinal ulcers from forming. It will help you to manage stress more effectively.

Step three in the yogic approach to good health, which embraces a health-promoting diet, is described in the next chapter.

CHAPTER THREE

HEALING NUTRIENTS

Nutrition aims at promoting and maintaining good health, and rebuilding it when it has broken down. It is often a slow process; seldom as quick and dramatic, for example, as preventing the spread of infection with antibiotics. Studies indicate, however, that repairing the body through nutrition can be much more rapid than was formerly believed.

It is essentially what we eat that supplies the raw material for building and repairing the body's various components. Nutrients from the diet are processed by the digestive system and transported to every cell, tissue and organ through the circulatory system.

When there is a wound or infection, the body's demand for certain nutrients increases. As healing occurs, the body uses up nutrients at a greater rate than usual, as it does under other forms of stress. But it is as well to bear in mind that *all* nutrients work together for the harmonious functioning of the entire system.

If you are considering taking nutritional supplements, please first consult a nutritionist, a dietitian or other qualified health professional. Some vitamins and minerals taken indiscriminately can be toxic.

Here are some guidelines on nutrients that are essential for healthy living, including information on the food sources from which they may be obtained. Please note that although mention has been made of deficiency diseases such as beriberi and scurvy, these are now virtually nonexistent in the West. They have been included in this chapter, however, for general information on the role of vitamins in the diet.

VITAMINS

Vitamin A (Retinol)

Vitamin A is essential for maintaining healthy hair, skin and the mucous membranes that line body cavities and tubular organs. It is helpful in treating acne. Formerly known as the 'anti-infection' vitamin', vitamin A builds resistance to infections such as respiratory diseases. It is necessary for counteracting night blindness and weak eyesight, and helps in the treatment of several eye disorders. Useful in the treatment of an overactive thyroid gland, it also promotes the growth of strong bones, and protects the lining of joints against inflammation. Like vitamins C and E, vitamin A is an antioxidant: it averts certain types of oxygen damage.

Vitamin A deficiency may result in skin, hair and nail problems, and in problems of the digestive, urinary and respiratory systems. It leads to an increased susceptibility to infections and certain eye problems (including night blindness), and in fatigue and low energy.

Good vitamin A sources include: fresh vegetables, especially the intensely green and yellow ones such as asparagus, broccoli, carrots, dandelion leaves, kale, parsley, spinach, squash, sweet potatoes and turnip tops; fresh fruits, especially apricots, cantaloupe melons, cherries, mangoes, papaya and peaches; milk and milk products, and fish liver oils.

Carotenoids (Carotenes)

Carotenes represent the most widespread group of naturally occurring pigments in plant life. Many people equate the term 'carotene' with pro-vitamin A, but only 30–50 of the more than 400 carotenoids are believed to have vitamin A activity.

Recent evidence indicates that carotenes have many more activities than serving simply as a vitamin A precursor. Although research has focused primarily on betacarotene, other carotenes are more potent in their antioxidant activity, and are deposited in tissues to a greater degree.

Foods rich in betacarotene are also rich in the many other carotenoids. A high intake of these substances is associated with a reduced rate of cancers involving epithelial cells (lungs, skin, cervix, respiratory tract, gastrointestinal tract, and so on). The consumption of foods rich in carotenes (such as green leafy vegetables, yams, sweet potatoes, carrots, broccoli, squash, cantaloupe melons and apricots) offers significant benefits to the immune system.

The B Vitamins

Called 'the nerve vitamins', this complex consists of more than 20 vitamins, essential for maintaining a healthy nervous system and for helping counteract the harmful effects of stress. In addition, they help build and repair the body's cells to produce healthy skin, hair and nails. The B vitamins affect all components of the immune system, which protects us from threats of infection and other forms of disease.

Deficiency of any of the B vitamins can result in low energy levels. The harder you work and the less sleep you get, the greater is your need for these vitamins.

The B-complex vitamins are present in brewer's yeast, green leafy vegetables, legumes (dried peas, beans and lentils), wheat germ and whole grains and cereals.

The individual vitamins within the B complex are as follows:

B1 (Thiamine)

Thiamine is important for growth. It aids appetite, and is necessary for proper digestion, especially that of carbohydrates. It is essential for normal functioning of nervous tissue, and keeps muscles (including the heart muscle) functioning normally. It helps combat travel sickness, and it has been found useful in relieving postoperative pain.

Thiamine deficiency results in a loss of appetite, impaired digestion, irritable bowel syndrome, constipation and diarrhoea. It can cause various types of nervous disorder and a loss of the coordination power of muscles, as well as fatigue and weakness. Thiamine deficiency may also produce beriberi, early symptoms of which include: fatigue, irritability, poor memory, sleep disturbance, loss of appetite, constipation and abdominal discomfort.

Good thiamine sources include: brazil nuts, brewer's yeast, buckwheat flour, cantaloupe melons, green leafy vegetables, legumes, potatoes, rolled oats, soya beans, sunflower seeds, whole grains and yellow cornmeal.

B₂ (Riboflavin)

Riboflavin is important for the formation of certain enzymes. It aids growth and reproduction, and promotes healthy skin, hair and nails. It helps prevent or heal a sore mouth, tongue and lips. It eases eye fatigue and benefits vision.

Riboflavin deficiency may result in weakness, anaemia, impaired growth, skin problems, intolerance of light (photophobia), inflamed tongue, cracks at the corners of the mouth (cheilosis), and a lowered resistance to infection.

Good riboflavin sources include: almonds, brewer's yeast, broccoli, buckwheat flour, cantaloupe melons, dark green leafy vegetables, legumes, lima beans, milk and milk products, mushrooms, sunflower seeds, wheat germ, whole grains and wild rice.

B₃ (Niacin, Nicotinic Acid, Nicotinamide)

Vitamin B_3 is considered an antioxidant, much like vitamins A, C and E. It helps to promote a healthy digestive system and to alleviate disturbances of the stomach and intestines. Other vitamin B_3 roles include: promoting healthy skin; helping prevent and ease the severity of migraine headaches; improving blood circulation; reducing cholesterol and high blood pressure; helping counteract the unpleasant symptoms of vertigo; assisting the healing of canker sores; and sometimes combating bad breath. It also increases energy as it promotes the body's proper utilization of food.

(Note that nicotinic acid, *not* nicotinamide, causes a widening of blood vessels and consequent flushing.)

Vitamin B_3 deficiency can result in weakness, digestive disorders, irritability, depression and pellagra – characterized by skin, stomach, intestinal and nervous symptoms.

Good vitamin B_3 sources include: artichokes, asparagus, brewer's yeast, green leafy vegetables, legumes, nuts, potatoes, seeds, whole grains and whole-grain products.

B₅ (Pantothenic Acid, Pantothenol, Calcium Pantothenate)

Vitamin B_5 enhances immunity to disease. It helps wounds to heal, and is useful in preventing fatigue and increasing energy. It counteracts skin inflammations, and is important for the normal functioning of adrenal gland secretions, which play a vital role in stress reactions.

A vitamin B_5 deficiency may produce low blood sugar (hypoglycaemia), duodenal ulcers, fatigue and blood and skin disorders. When vitamin B_5 is deficient in the diet, fats burn at only half their normal rate – a fact worth remembering when you are trying to lose weight and increase energy.

Vitamin B_5 may be obtained from the following: avocados, brewer's yeast, broccoli, brown rice, cabbage, cauliflower, filbert nuts, green vegetables, legumes, milk, mushrooms, pecan nuts, potatoes, sunflower seeds, sweet potatoes, tomatoes, unrefined vegetable oils, wheat germ and whole grains.

B₆ (Pyridoxine)

Pyridoxine is important for maintaining a good resistance to disease. It is needed for the proper assimilation of protein and fat, and for the production of hormones. It aids in the conversion of tryptophan (an essential amino acid) to niacin, helps prevent various nervous and skin disorders, and alleviates nausea. It also promotes the synthesis of anti-ageing nucleic acids, and is helpful in reducing leg cramps, nocturnal muscle spasms, hand numbness and certain nerve inflammations of the extremities. An additional role for vitamin B_6 is as a natural diuretic (an agent that increases the secretion of urine).

A pyridoxine deficiency can result in anaemia, dandruff, skin problems, inflamed nerves, loss of appetite, nausea, vomiting and an inflamed tongue.

Good pyridoxine sources include: apples, asparagus, avocados, bananas, blackstrap molasses, brewer's yeast, brown rice, buckwheat flour, cabbage, cantaloupe melons, carrots, eggs, filbert nuts, green leafy vegetables, milk, peas, prunes, raisins, sunflower seeds, tomatoes, wheat germ, whole grains and whole-grain products.

B9 (Folate, Folacin, Folic Acid)

Vitamin B_9 is essential for the normal functioning of the system responsible for the production and development of blood cells. It plays an important role in keeping the immune system working effectively, and can be useful as a pain reliever. Used in conjunction with vitamin B_5 and PABA (para-aminobenzoic acid), it may delay the greying of hair.

A vitamin B_9 deficiency can cause anaemia, two symptoms of which are fatigue and shortness of breath. It can also affect the proper formation of the body's disease-fighting cells, and be a contributing factor in excessive hair loss.

Good vitamin B_9 sources include: apricots, avocados, beans, carrots, egg yolk, green leafy vegetables, green onions, pumpkin, tempeh (a sort of cheese made from fermented soya beans), torula yeast, wheat germ and whole-grain products.

B12 (Cobalamin, Cyano-cobalamin)

Vitamin B_{12} is essential for the production and regeneration of red blood cells. It helps maintain a healthy nervous system and is useful for improving memory, concentration and balance. It is important for the body's

proper utilization of fats, carbohydrates and protein, and may also have a regulating effect on the immune system. Women may find this nutrient helpful just before and during menstruation.

Vitamin B_{12} deficiency may result in anaemia or in brain damage. Good food sources include eggs, milk products and tempeh. It is also synthesized by intestinal bacteria.

B15 (Pangamic Acid)

Vitamin B_{15} extends the life span of cells. It helps to lower blood cholesterol levels and relieve the symptoms of angina pectoris and asthma. It protects against pollutants, helps to prevent cirrhosis of the liver, neutralizes the craving for alcohol and helps to fend off hangovers. Vitamin B_{15} speeds recovery from fatigue, stimulates immunity responses and assists in protein synthesis.

Vitamin B_{15} deficiency may be linked to glandular and nervous disorders, heart disease and diminished oxygenation of tissues.

This vitamin may be obtained from brewer's yeast, brown rice, pumpkin seeds, sesame seeds and whole grains.

Biotin (Coenzyme R, Vitamin H)

Biotin is associated with the vitamin B complex and is necessary for the body's effective utilization of this group of vitamins. Important for carbohydrate metabolism, it is needed for a healthy nervous system, and can help prevent hair from turning grey and from falling out excessively. It is also useful for alleviating skin inflammations and muscle pains.

A biotin deficiency could result in eczema of the face and body, loss of appetite, insomnia, irritability, depression and extreme exhaustion.

Good biotin sources include brewer's

yeast, brown rice, egg yolk, fresh fruits, legumes, nuts, wheat germ and whole grains.

Choline

Choline is another member of the vitamin B complex. It helps control the build-up of cholesterol, and aids in the transmission of nerve impulses, especially those involved with memory. It helps to eliminate poisons and drugs from the system through the liver.

A choline deficiency may lead to liver disorders, a hardening of the arteries and possibly Alzheimer's disease.

Good choline sources include egg yolk, green leafy vegetables, lecithin and wheat germ.

Inositol

Inositol is yet another member of the vitamin B complex. It can help lower cholesterol levels, promote healthy hair and prevent excessive hair loss. It may help counteract eczema and be useful in the redistribution of body fat. It also aids in preventing constipation.

Inositol deficiency may result in eczema and contribute to abnormal hair loss (alopecia).

The best natural sources of inositol include: brewer's yeast, cabbage, cantaloupe melons, grapefruit, lima beans (dried), molasses (unrefined), peanuts, raisins and wheat germ.

PABA (Para-aminobenzoic Acid)

This member of the vitamin B complex is important for healthy intestines, effective metabolism, and the proper formation of blood cells. It can help to keep skin healthy and to delay wrinkles, and has been known to aid in restoring natural colour to the hair. Used as an ointment, it is helpful for protection against sunburn.

PABA deficiency symptoms include fatigue, digestive disorders, headaches, nervousness, depression and constipation. PABA deficiency can also result in eczema and the greying of hair.

Like other B-complex vitamins, PABA is supplied by brewer's yeast, eggs, green leafy vegetables, molasses, rice bran (rice polish), wheat germ, whole grains and yogurt.

Anti-stress Factors

Associated with the B complex, these are vitamin-like substances which have a protective action against the impact of various stressors. In clinical tests, laboratory rats subjected to chemical stressors (for example, aspirin and cortisone) suffered adverse reactions that could not be reversed through supplementation with certain nutrients. When given foods containing the anti-stress factors, however, they were found to be fully protected. Research suggests that those suffering from ill health benefit from incorporating into their diet as many foods as possible that contain these nutrients.

The anti-stress factors are found in green leafy vegetables, some nutritional yeasts, soya flour (from which the oil has not been removed) and wheat germ.

Vitamin C (Ascorbic Acid)

This vitamin is essential for the formation and maintenance of collagen – a cement-like substance that holds together the cells forming a variety of tissues including skin, cartilage and bone.

Vitamin C, an anti-stress vitamin, is needed to build resistance to disease and for various healing processes. It also contributes to the body's utilization of oxygen and to its maintenance of a healthy blood circulation. Like vitamins A and E, it is an antioxidant, helping to slow down the destructive effects of oxygen and other substances.

Other vitamin C roles include: helping to decrease blood cholesterol levels; reducing the incidence of blood clots in veins; aiding in the prevention and easing of symptoms of the common cold; reducing the effects of many allergy-producing substances; acting as a natural laxative. It also facilitates the absorption of iron.

Vitamin C deficiency may result in a lowered resistance to inrections; tender joints and a susceptibility to gum and tooth disease. If the deficiency is severe, anaemia or haemorrhage can occur; so can scurvy, which is characterized by bleeding and abnormal formation of the bones and teeth. (Scurvy is preceded by a period of ill health, and symptoms include loss of energy, sallow complexion, pain in the joints, 'iron-poor blood', bleeding gums and the loosening of teeth.)

The best vitamin C sources include: fresh fruits such as apricots, blackberries, blueberries, cantaloupe melons, cherries, elderberries, gooseberries, grapefruit, guavas, honeydew melons, kiwi fruit, kumquats, lemons, limes, oranges, papaya, rosehips and strawberries; and fresh vegetables such as cabbage, dandelion leaves, green and red peppers, kohlrabi, mustard and cress and turnip tops.

Flavonoids
Associated with vitamin C, these compounds – responsible for the colours of fruits and flowers – offer remarkable protection against free radical damage. (Free radicals are molecules produced by oxidation during normal metabolic processes. They can damage the membranes and genetic material of cells, and have been implicated in cancerous tissue changes, heart and lung disease, cataracts and premature ageing.) While flavonoids protect plants against environmental stress, in humans they appear to function as biological response modifiers as indicated by their anti-inflammatory, anti-allergic, anti-viral and anti-carcinogenic activity.

Flavonoids increase the effectiveness of vitamin C; strengthen the walls of capillaries and veins; help build resistance to infection; prevent gums from bleeding and promote their healing; and are useful in the treatment of oedema (swelling) and dizziness from disease of the inner ear.

The best way to ensure an adequate intake of flavonoids is to eat a varied diet, rich in fresh fruits and vegetables.

Vitamin D (Calciferol)

Vitamin D regulates the absorption of calcium and phosphorus from the intestines and assists in the assimilation of vitamin A. Taken with vitamins A and C, it can help prevent colds. It is also useful in treating conjunctivitis, an inflammation of the mucous membrane that lines the eyelids.

Mild vitamin-D deficiency interferes with the body's utilization of calcium in bone and teeth formation. In children a severe deficiency may lead to rickets, (which results in abnormal bone development); and in adults to osteomalacia, (in which bones soften) and senile osteoporosis (in which there is increased bone porosity in later life).

Our most reliable vitamin D source is vitamin D-enriched milk; but butter, eggs and fish liver oils provide small amounts. Plant foods contain no vitamin D.

Vitamin E (Tocopherol)

Vitamin E, one of the anti-stress vitamins, is an active antioxidant; it prevents oxidation of vitamin A, selenium, some vitamin C and fat compounds. It also enhances vitamin A activity.

Vitamin E plays an important role as a vasodilator (an agent that widens blood vessels), and thus improves circulation. As an anti-coagulant, it dissolves and helps prevent blood clots. It also works as a diuretic, increasing the flow of urine; and it can lower high blood pressure.

Vitamin E can help keep you looking younger by slowing down cellular ageing resulting from oxidation. It helps supply oxygen to the body, improving levels of endurance and alleviating fatigue. Along with vitamin C, it can protect lungs against air pollution. Vitamin E may prevent ugly scar formation if taken internally and applied to the area involved by piercing the ends of a vitamin E capsule and squeezing the oil onto it. It can also accelerate the healing of burns, aid in preventing miscarriages, and help ease unpleasant menopausal symptoms.

Vitamin E deficiency may result in the destruction of red blood cells and some forms of anaemia. It may be a factor in certain reproductive disorders, and in kidney and liver damage.

Good vitamin E sources include: almonds and other nuts, broccoli, Brussels sprouts, eggs, fresh fruits, green leafy vegetables, legumes, seeds, unrefined vegetable oils, wheat germ and whole grains.

EFAs (Essential Fatty Acids, Polyunsaturated Fatty Acids)

Two classes of fatty acids are considered essential (essential, in this case, means that our body needs them but cannot produce them, so we require them from foods.) These are the omega-3 and omega-6 fatty acids.

EFAs are a vital part of the structure of every cell in the body. They are also a necessary component of the fatty film that coats the skin's surface, a film that is important for protection against the entry of disease-causing organisms.

EFAs play a role in cholesterol metabolism and in blood clotting. They help provide energy, maintain body temperature, insulate nerves, cushion and protect tissues, and promote healthy skin, hair and nails. EFAs, moreover, aid in weight reduction by burning saturated fats.

EFA deficiency may result in acne and eczema. Other deficiency symptoms include: poor reproductive capacity; heart and blood-circulation disorders; faulty healing of wounds; dried-up tear ducts and salivary glands; lowered resistance to infections; improper formation of collagen and abnormal hair loss.

Generally the best sources of EFAs are the

ESSENTIAL VITAMINS

A (retinol)	B_9 (folic acid)	C (ascorbic acid)
B complex:	B_{12} (cobalamin)	D (calciferol)
B_1 (thiamine)	B_{15} (pangamic acid)	E (tocopherol)
B_2 (riboflavin)	Biotin	EFAs (essential fatty
B_3 (niacin)	Choline	acids)
B_5 (pantothenic acid)	Inositol	K (menadione)
B_6 (pyridoxone)	PABA (para-	
	aminobenzoic acid)	

oils of certain seeds and nuts, such as flax seed, sunflower, sesame and evening primrose. Other good sources include: wheat germ, soya bean and peanut oils, almonds, avocados, peanuts, pecans, sunflower seeds and walnuts. (Although most nuts provide some EFAs, brazil and cashew nuts do not.)

Vitamin K (Menadione, Menaphthone)

Also known as 'the blood vitamin', vitamin K promotes proper blood clotting and helps to prevent bleeding. It also aids in reducing excessive menstrual flow.

A vitamin K deficiency could result in colitis (inflammation of the large intestine) and sprue, (symptoms of which include weakness, weight loss and various digestive disorders).

A varied, wholesome diet generally provides an adequate supply of vitamin K for normal requirements. Rich food sources, however, include: alfalfa sprouts, cow's milk, egg yolk, fish liver oils, green leafy vegetables and kelp; also safflower, soya bean and other unrefined vegetable oils.

MINERALS

Boron

The trace mineral boron has been shown to safeguard calcium in the body. It appears to be necessary for activating vitamin D, as well as certain hormones, including oestrogen. Boron, moreover, elevates the concentration of the most biologically active form of oestrogen in the blood – oestrogen administration has proved to be effective for slowing calcium loss from bone in postmenopausal women.

Fresh fruits and vegetables are the main sources of boron. These include: alfalfa, cabbage, lettuce, peas, snap beans, apples and grapes; also soya beans, dates, prunes and raisins. Boron may also be obtained from almonds, hazelnuts and peanuts.

Note: Since the human requirement for boron has not yet been established, and the results of long-term toxicity studies have yet to be reported, boron supplementation is *not* recommended. You can increase boron intake, however, by including boron-rich foods in your diet.

Calcium

Considered an anti-stress mineral, calcium is needed for the proper functioning of nervous tissue, for good muscle tone, normal blood clotting and for the maintenance of sound bones and healthy teeth. Calcium is required to keep your heart beating regularly. It helps metabolize your body's iron and can aid in combating insomnia. It is also needed to maintain a sound chemical balance in the body. In order for calcium to be absorbed, vitamin D supplies must be adequate. Vitamin C and lactose (milk sugar) enhance calcium absorption.

Emotional stress and prolonged bed rest increase calcium requirements; so do high-fat and high-protein diets. Calcium deficiency results in the wasting of energy, an inability to relax and can also lead to rickets, osteomalacia and osteoporosis.

The best food sources of calcium include: blackstrap molasses, carob flour (powder), citrus fruits, dried beans, dried figs, green vegetables, milk and milk products, peanuts, sesame seeds, soya beans, sunflower seeds and walnuts.

Chlorine

This mineral aids digestion and is essential for the formation of hydrochloric acid in the stomach. It helps keep you limber since it aids in stimulating and regulating muscular action.

A chlorine deficiency may contribute to the loss of hair and teeth.

The best natural sources of chlorine include kelp and olives.

Chromium

Useful in helping to prevent and to lower high blood pressure, chromium also works as a preventive against diabetes.

Chromium deficiency is suspected to be a factor in arteriosclerosis (the hardening of arteries) and diabetes.

The best natural chromium sources include brewer's yeast and corn oil. Refined foods are often stripped of chromium.

Cobalt

Cobalt is part of vitamin B_{12} and is, therefore, essential for red blood cells. It also helps in preventing anaemia.

A cobalt deficiency can result in anaemia and its associated loss of energy.

Good natural cobalt sources include green leafy vegetables, kelp, torula yeast and whole grains grown on mineral-rich soils.

Copper

Copper is an essential trace mineral which plays an important role in many enzyme systems. It helps in the development and functioning of nerve, brain and connective tissue. It is needed in small amounts to help synthesize haemoglobin – the colouring matter of red blood cells, which is often low in anaemia. It is also required to convert the body's iron into haemoglobin and is essential for the utilization of vitamin C.

Copper deficiency decreases the absorption of iron and shortens the life span of red blood cells. These deficiencies contribute to anaemia. A copper deficiency may also lead to oedema (swelling).

If you eat an adequate supply of green leafy vegetables and whole-grain products, it is unlikely that you will have to worry about copper deficiency. Other food sources of this nutrient are legumes, nuts and prunes.

Fluorine (Fluoride)

This mineral is vital to general wellbeing. It works with calcium to strengthen bones and is also important for sound teeth.

Fluoride deficiency may lead to tooth decay.

Organic fluorine is found in almonds, beetroot tops, carrots, garlic, green vegetables, milk and cheese, steel-cut oats and sunflower seeds. It is normally present in sea water and in naturally hard water.

Iodine (Iodide)

Iodine can help with weight control by burning excess fat. It contributes to the maintenance of good energy levels, helps maintain mental alertness, and promotes healthy hair, skin, nails and teeth.

Two-thirds of the body's iodine is in the thyroid gland. Since this gland controls metabolism, an under-supply of iodine can result in slow mental reaction, lack of energy and weight gain. Iodine deficiency can also lead to goitre – an enlargement of the thyroid gland, which is still not uncommon in areas where the soil is iodine deficient. (Symptoms of goitre include rapid heartbeat, nervous irritability and anaemia).

The best natural sources of iodine include: broccoli, cabbage, carrots, garlic, lettuce, onion, pineapple and foods grown in iodine-rich, coastal soils.

Iron

Iron is required for the proper metabolism of the B vitamins and, together with the minerals cobalt, copper and manganese, is necessary for the assimilation of vitamin C.

Iron is a vital component of haemoglobin, which transports oxygen to all body cells. It is, moreover, an essential part of immune system enzymes and proteins, and important for the vitality of germ-killing cells. Vitamin C facilitates the absorption of iron.

An iron deficiency leads to anaemia.

Perhaps the greatest single cause of iron deficiency is the refining of breads, cereals and sugar. Although iron is added to so-called enriched flour, this food item is *not* a rich source compared, for example, with brewer's yeast and wheat germ. Other commendable food sources of iron include: artichokes, asparagus, blackstrap molasses, Brussels sprouts, cauliflower, dried fruits, egg yolk, kiwi fruit, leafy vegetables, seaweed, seeds, sharon fruit (persimmon), strawberries, watermelon and whole grains.

Caution. Unless you are a menstruating woman or have suffered a significant loss of blood, you should not take iron supplements except as prescribed by your doctor, following suitable blood tests that reveal an iron-deficiency anaemia. Excess iron can accumulate in the body to toxic levels, which can interfere with immunity and possibly promote cancer. If you take a multivitamin and/or multimineral supplement, make sure it contains *no iron* – unless iron has been prescribed for you.

Magnesium

Magnesium is needed by every cell in the body since it is essential for the body's synthesis of protein and for the utilization of fats, the B vitamins and several minerals. It acts as an important catalyst in many enzyme reactions: most of these enzymes contain vitamin B_6, which is not well absorbed unless magnesium is adequately provided by the diet.

Known as an anti-stress mineral, magnesium aids in combating depression and in promoting a healthy cardiovascular system (heart and blood vessels). It helps to keep teeth healthy and to prevent the formation of stones in the kidneys and gall bladder. It can also relieve indigestion.

Alcoholics are usually deficient in magnesium. The symptoms of magnesium deficiency include: fatigue, weakness, nervous tension and insomnia. These are often remedied when magnesium is supplied. In fact, magnesium may be regarded as one of nature's tranquillizers.

The milling of grains – with the consequent removal of the bran and germ – has substantially affected magnesium intake. White flour, for instance, has only 22 per cent of the magnesium present in whole-wheat flour. The best magnesium sources include: alfalfa sprouts, almonds and other nuts eaten fresh from the shell, apples, beetroot tops, blackstrap molasses, brown rice, celery, chard, dried fruits (including figs), grapefruit, green leafy vegetables grown on mineral-rich soils, oranges, peas, potatoes, sesame seeds, soya beans, sunflower seeds, wheat bran, wheat germ and whole grains.

Manganese

Manganese helps activate enzymes necessary for the body's proper use of biotin, vitamin B_1 and vitamin C. It is needed for sound bone structure and for the formation of thyroxin, the principal hormone of the thyroid gland.

Manganese is required for the proper digestion and utilization of food, and is important for the normal functioning of the nervous and reproductive systems. Because of its role in these vital body functions, manganese can help reduce fatigue and irritability, and improve memory.

The best natural manganese sources include: beets, egg yolk, green leafy vegetables, nuts, peas and whole-grain cereals.

Molybdenum

This mineral forms a vital part of the enzyme responsible for the body's iron utilization. It can help prevent anaemia and promote general wellbeing.

Molybdenum deficiency may contribute to dental caries, male impotence, irritability and an irregular heartbeat.

The best food source of this nutrient includes dark-green leafy vegetables, legumes and whole grains.

Phosphorus

Phosphorus works with calcium to build bones and teeth. It helps maintain normal brain and nerve tissue.

A phosphorus deficiency results in weight loss, loss of appetite, irregular breathing and fatigue.

Food sources of phosphorus include: corn, dairy products (low-fat), dried fruits, egg yolks, legumes, nuts, seeds and whole grains.

Potassium

Together with the mineral sodium, potassium helps maintain the electrical and chemical balance between tissue cells and the blood. These two nutrients must be in balance in order to maintain muscle contractions and the normal transmission of nerve signals.

Potassium plays an important part in the release of energy from carbohydrates, proteins and fats. When the sodium level is high in proportion to that of potassium, health problems such as muscle weakness, mental confusion and heart disorders may occur.

Potassium can contribute to clear thinking by facilitating the supply of oxygen to the brain. It can help dispose of body wastes, reduce high blood pressure and enhance allergy treatment.

Low blood sugar (hypoglycaemia) causes potassium loss, as does severe diarrhoea or a long fast. Both mental and physical stress can lead to potassium deficiency, which may result in oedema (swelling) and in hypoglycaemia.

Foods in their natural state offer the best sources of potassium, without being too high in sodium. These include: bananas, cereals (whole grain), citrus fruit, green leafy vegetables, legumes, mint leaves, nuts, potatoes, watercress and watermelon.

Selenium

Selenium is a trace mineral needed to maintain healthy circulation and to reinforce the body's immune system. It works with vitamins C and E to help detoxify the body and keep it free of harmful substances (selenium is an antioxidant). It may play a part in neutralizing certain cancer-producing agents.

Men appear to have a greater need for selenium than women. Almost half of their body's supply concentrates in the testicles and parts of the seminal ducts near the prostate gland. Selenium is lost in semen.

Selenium helps preserve the youthful elasticity of tissues. It can ease hot flushes and other discomforts of menopause. It is also useful in preventing and treating dandruff.

Selenium deficiency may result in loss of stamina.

The best food sources of this nutrient include: apple cider vinegar, asparagus, brewer's yeast, eggs, garlic, mushrooms, sesame seeds, unrefined cereals, wheat germ, whole grains and whole-grain products.

Silicon (Silica)

Some skin experts say that this trace mineral gives life to the skin, lustre to the hair and beautiful finishing touches to the whole body.

Silicon is essential for both the hardness and flexibility of bones. It hastens the healing of fractures, reduces scarring at fracture sites, and contributes to the building up of connective tissue. It is also required for the normal functioning of the adrenal glands which are involved in stress reactions.

Foods made from natural buckwheat are a rich source of this micro-nutrient. Other sources include: apples, asparagus, barley, beets, brown rice, carrots, celery, cherries, corn, eggs, green leafy vegetables, green and red peppers, lentils, lettuce, millet, mushrooms, oats, onions, pears, potatoes, parsley, pumpkin, rye, strawberries, tomatoes and whole wheat.

Sodium

Sodium is necessary to preserve a balance between calcium and potassium in order to maintain normal heart action and the equilibrium of the body. It regulates body fluids (sodium, potassium and chlorine play an important role in keeping body fluids near a neutral pH).

Sodium-deficiency symptoms include weakness, nerve disorders, weight loss and disturbed digestion.

Natural sodium sources include: asparagus, beets, carrots, celery, courgettes (zucchini), egg yolks (raw), figs, marrow (squash), oatmeal, string beans and turnips.

Sulphur

Sulphur is essential for the formation of body tissues and is also needed for tissue respiration. It is part of the vitamin B complex and is required for collagen synthesis. Known as 'the beauty mineral', sulphur helps keep the hair glossy and the complexion clear.

Food sources of sulphur include: beans, bran, Brussels sprouts, cabbage, egg yolks, garlic, horseradish, kale, onions, peppers (all kinds) and radishes.

Vanadium

This trace mineral may be related to the regulation of electrolytes (such as sodium, potassium and chlorine) inside and outside the body's cells, which influence the storage of excess food calories as fat. Even a marginal vanadium deficiency may slow down this process and lower the fuel-burning rate. The net effect of this could be an inexplicable gain in weight. Vanadium also inhibits cholesterol formation and is important for the development of bones, cartilage and teeth.

Vanadium is found primarily in plant foods (radish is one source) and in unrefined foods.

Zinc

One of the keys to good health, zinc is a vital component of the immune system which protects us from disease (it is an anti-viral agent). It is intricately involved in tissue nutrition and repair, and speeds up the healing of internal and external wounds.

ESSENTIAL MINERALS

Boron	Iodine	Selenium
Calcium	Iron	Silicon
Chlorine	Magnesium	Sodium
Chromium	Manganese	Sulphur
Cobalt	Molybedenum	Vanadium
Copper	Phosphorus	Zinc
Fluorine	Potassium	

Zinc is essential for the proper functioning of more than 70 enzyme systems. It is a constituent of an indispensable enzyme called carbonic anhydrase, which removes carbon dioxide from tissues. It is also necessary for the assimilation of the B vitamins which are crucial to general well-being.

This mineral is needed at every age and stage of life, from conception to old age. It is involved in all aspects of reproduction and can help in preventing prostate gland problems and in treating infertility. Zinc, moreover, can aid in preventing loss of taste, promote mental alertness and reduce cholesterol deposits in blood vessels. It is also needed for healthy skin and nails.

A zinc deficiency can have widespread results because of the many and varied roles this mineral plays. Disorders linked to an under-supply of zinc include: non-cancerous enlargement of the prostate gland, arteriosclerosis and a lowered resistance to infection. Women bothered by menstrual irregularities might also do well to consider zinc supplementation before resorting to hormonal treatments to establish regular periods.

Foods rich in zinc include: brewer's yeast, cheese, eggs, broad (lima) beans, green beans, mushrooms, non-fat dry milk, nuts, pumpkin seeds, soya beans, sunflower seeds, wheat germ and whole-grain products.

OTHER NUTRIENTS

Dietary fibre

Dietary fibre is essential for preventing constipation, symptoms of which include general malaise, fatigue and loss of energy. Studies have shown that there is a much lower incidence of health disorders such as varicose veins, haemorrhoids (piles), high cholesterol, gall stones and obesity among people whose diet is high in fibre than among those who habitually eat low-fibre foods.

Dietary fibre exists only in vegetables, breads, cereal products, fruits, grains, legumes, nuts and seeds. The major categories of dietary fibre are pectin, found in apples and other fruits, citrus peel, marmalade and jams; cellulose, the stringy fibre in vegetables which is also found in cereal foods, fruits, grains, nuts and seeds; and hemi-cellulose, consisting of a number of related substances, found in cereal and cereal products, fruits, nuts, seeds and vegetables. There are also gums, found in oats and legumes; and saponins, found in alfalfa, asparagus, chickpeas, aubergines (eggplant), kidney and mung beans, oats, peanuts, peas, soya beans, spinach and sunflower seeds.

Carnitine

There are two forms of carnitine: L-carnitine and D-carnitine. D-carnitine is the biologically inactive form of carnitine, while L-carnitine is the active form found in our tissues. L-carnitine is an amino acid (protein building block). Its main function is to transport fatty acids into the 'powerhouses' of tissue cells in order to generate energy.

Heart muscle contains a high level of carnitine. Medical trials have indicated that carnitine may be useful in protecting the heart muscle of people with clogged arteries. In one study, treatment with carnitine brought about improvement in tolerance of exercise. Other benefits noted in people taking carnitine supplements were an improved mental alertness and better muscle function in those suffering from intermittent claudication – a severe pain in the calf muscles during walking, which subsides with rest, and occurs because of an inadequate blood supply. Alcohol increases the need for carnitine. If you use carnitine supplements, however, use *only* L-carnitine.

Although L-carnitine is almost totally restricted to animal foods, humans do produce some from two essential amino acids, lysine and methionine. Three vitamins (B_3, B_6 and C) and iron are involved in this synthesis. Dairy products contain some carnitine, as do avocados and tempeh (a fermented soya bean product).

Lecithin

Lecithin breaks down cholesterol and fats in the blood, allowing them to be effectively utilized by the body's cells. Other nutrients vital for lecithin production are vitamin B_6, choline, inositol and magnesium. If your diet is adequate and provides a sufficient amount of these nutrients, you can produce all the lecithin your body needs.

All unrefined foods containing oil provide lecithin. These include: nuts, soya beans and wheat. Eggs also contain lecithin (the lecithin content of a fertile egg is about 1700 mg).

NUTRIENT ANTAGONISTS

Agents that counteract the health-promoting properties of the minerals, vitamins and other nutrients in the food we eat are known as antagonists.

The following are among the most notorious nutrient antagonists: aspirin, which increases the need for vitamin C; oral contraceptive pills, which act against zinc and the B vitamins; rancid oils and other rancid foods, which destroy vitamin E; some commercial laxatives, notably mineral oil, which can cause deficiency of vitamin C and the B vitamins; smoking, which destroys vitamin C and the B vitamins and reduces vital oxygen supplies to tissues; high alcohol intake, which is antagonistic to several essential minerals and vitamins; too much caffeine, which adversely affects the circulatory and respiratory systems and contributes to dehydration; and lack of exercise, which impairs the delivery of vital nutrients to body tissues.

DIETARY SUGGESTIONS

- Reduce your intake of high-fat foods which contribute to heart and blood vessel diseases.
- Avoid high-protein diets which place extra demands on the body and can

increase the need for other nutrients.

- Ensure a regular intake of dietary fibre to help prevent disorders such as constipation, piles and varicose veins.
- Eat plenty of complex carbohydrates ('slowly-digested carbohydrates') such as whole grain breads and pasta, potatoes, and fresh fruit and vegetables, to provide important nutrients and bulk, to regulate bowel function and contribute to a trim, healthy body.
- Avoid using over-processed foods (including many convenience foods) which are often devoid of many essential nutrients.
- Reduce sodium (salt) added to food during preparation and cooking, and also at the table. High sodium intake has been linked to high blood pressure.
- Cut down consumption of refined sugars which have been implicated in conditions such as tooth decay, obesity, diabetes and high cholesterol levels.
- Decrease or eliminate your caffeine intake. Instead, drink beverages such as water, unsweetened fruit juices, freshly pressed vegetable juices, herbal teas and milk.
- Consume less or avoid any substances known to be antagonistic to essential nutrients, such as alcohol, cigarette smoke and commercial laxatives.
- If you are troubled by symptoms of low blood sugar (hypoglycaemia), replace your regular three large meals with five or six small wholesome meals evenly spaced throughout the day, to help maintain adequate blood sugar levels.
- Store, prepare and cook food in ways that conserve nutrients.
- Try to make mealtimes pleasant and unhurried, and do not overeat.

PART TWO

THE EXERCISES

CHAPTER FOUR ⟡

PREPARING FOR THE EXERCISES

Yoga exercises are to be done with complete awareness, in synchronization with breathing. Practised in this way, they are safe and effective. It is not possible, however, to cover all eventualities in this book. Before attempting the postures and other exercises, therefore, please *check with your doctor*. He or she will be able to advise you as to whether or not they are safe for *you* to do and compatible with any treatment you may be having. This advice also applies to any particular technique about which you are uncertain. Be equally cautious if you have a serious health problem or have had surgery of any kind.

COMFORT AND HYGIENE

Remove from your person any object that might injure you, such as glasses, hair ornaments or jewellery. Wear loose, comfortable clothing that permits you to move and breathe freely. Practise bare-footed whenever possible.

For maximum comfort, empty your bladder, and possibly also your bowel, before starting yoga practice. If you wish, you may take a warm (*not* hot) bath or shower before exercising, especially if you feel particularly stiff. Attend, as well, to oral and nasal hygiene. (Please refer to Chapter 9 for suggestions.)

WHEN TO PRACTISE

Try to do the exercises at about the same time every day (or at least every other day) on a regular basis.

Practising in the morning helps reduce stiffness after many hours spent in bed and gives you energy for your day. Practice in the evening produces a pleasant fatigue and promotes sound sleep. If you find, however that practising in the evening is too stimulating and prevents you from falling asleep easily, then try instead to fit your exercises in where they seem most convenient and beneficial.

If you plan a session of breathing exercises (*pranayama*) separate from the physical exercises (*asanas*), make it about 15 minutes after doing the simpler *asanas*, or about an hour before. You may also plan two 15-minute or half-hour sessions a day, or every other day: warm-ups and other exercises in the morning, and breathing and meditative exercises in the evening.

FITTING EXERCISES INTO THE WORK DAY

Several of the exercises such as the neck, shoulder and ankle warm-ups (*see Chapter 5*), and some of the breathing techniques (*see Chapter 7*), can be done at convenient times throughout your work day to prevent a build-up of tension. For example, you can tighten your abdominal muscles as you exhale while sitting at a desk or standing in a queue at the bank. You can rotate your ankles while watching television, with your legs elevated. You can slow down your breathing and make it smoother and deeper while driving in difficult traffic conditions, to help you keep calm.

FOOD AND DRINK

Yoga exercises are best practised on an empty or near-empty stomach. The best time for practice is before breakfast. In any case, allow two or three hours to elapse after a meal, depending on its size and content. You may practise an hour after eating a light snack.

If you find the above difficult or inconvenient, you may drink a cup of tea or other non-alcoholic beverage prior to exercising.

RESTARTING AFTER A BREAK

When you restart yoga practice after a period of interruption, do so in a very gradual way. Begin with the simplest, gentlest exercises and slowly progress towards the most challenging. Do *not* try to make up for lost time by overexerting yourself. Be patient.

SETTING THE SCENE

In some forms of exercise, it is not unusual to be 'working out' while thinking of unrelated matters: what you are going to cook for dinner tomorrow; what you are going to wear to the office party; or how you are to meet a deadline. This is *not* encouraged when practising yoga. Without the appropriate mental setting, yoga exercises will have no lasting value. For the restoration and maintenance of good health, you need to approach yoga practice with an attitude of calm and positive anticipation.

When you arrive at the place where you are going to do your yoga practice, leave behind you any cares or concerns; any grudges, resentments or other negative feelings. Before starting the exercises, spend a minute or two sitting still, with eyes closed, in quiet contemplation. You might, for example, reflect on one or two things for which to be thankful. You might simply turn your attention to your breathing and, if it is rapid and shallow, consciously slow it down by taking several deep breaths (as deep as possible in the circumstances, without straining) in smooth succession. You might do a quick mental check of your body – from head to toe – and wilfully let go of any tightness you may detect: in your jaws, hands, shoulders or elsewhere. You might, alternatively, silently recite some inspirational saying, such as 'I will leave disorder behind me. I will cultivate serenity.' 'I will be calm and in control.' The general aim is to quieten your body and divert your mind from usual concerns, in preparation for the yoga programme ahead.

WHERE TO PRACTISE

Choose a quiet, well-ventilated room with soft lighting. Because concentration is crucial to the effectiveness of yoga techniques, arrange to be undisturbed for the expected duration of your practice.

Practise on an even surface, and if the

room is not carpeted, place a non-skid mat on the floor on which to do your exercises. Whenever possible, practise outdoors, on a patio or a lawn on which a mat is spread.

From now on I shall refer to the surface on which you practise as the 'mat'.

HOW TO PRACTISE

One characteristic of popular exercise programmes of the past (and even of some current ones) was the ever-increasing number of times an exercise was repeated, and the decrease in the resting period between them. Relaxation, which is a significant component of muscle activity, was thus neglected.

Multiple repetitions of an exercise tend to produce fatigue and stiffness. Instead of tiresome repetitions, therefore, you can come back to a specific exercise later, or try a more advanced variation of it, or experiment with different combinations to exercise all muscle groups. Alternatively, you can give extra attention to areas of your body that need additional strengthening.

Rest periods and breathing appropriately are as important as the postures themselves. Doing the exercises *slowly and with complete awareness* ensures control of your position and movement at all times, and helps prevent injury. These principles are inherent in the yogic approach to exercise, an approach that represents centuries of wisdom.

COUNTER POSTURES

As a general rule, a backwards-bending posture should be balanced by a forwards-bending one, and vice versa. For example, after practising The Cobra (*page 57*) you could do the Pose of a Child (*page 55*). The Back-stretching Posture (*page 53*) may be followed by the Pelvic Stretch (*page 56*).

WARMING-UP

Always begin by warming-up (*see Chapter 5*), and give full attention to what you are doing. This has already been mentioned, but it is worth repeating since it is one of the things that make yoga techniques so effective in the restoration and maintenance of good health.

VISUALIZATION

Visualize the completed exercise. This is your goal, but not necessarily one that you must reach today. What really matters is the attempt to reach it and the diligence and perseverance that you bring to your practice. Try also to visualize the structures underneath the parts being exercised: for example, the organs, glands or blood and lymph vessels inside your body. Imagine them receiving an improved blood supply and their waste products being thoroughly eliminated.

BREATHING

Breathe regularly through your nostrils while doing an exercise (unless otherwise instructed). Do not hold your breath. Synchronize your breathing with the movement being performed. This allows delivery of oxygen to the working muscles and helps eliminate substances that cause fatigue. It also counteracts tension.

REPETITION AND REST

Except when doing warm-ups – in which several repetitions of an exercise in smooth succession are usual practice – do each exercise once or twice only (you can repeat it later), making your movements slow and conscious.

During the holding period (indicated in the exercise instructions as 'hold') *do not* simultaneously hold your breath; keep it flowing. Always rest briefly after each exercise, and check that you are breathing regularly.

When practising the seated postures, hold your spine naturally erect (but *not* rigid). Keep your facial muscles relaxed; unclench your teeth to relax your jaws. Breathe freely through your nostrils, except where otherwise indicated.

AFTER EXERCISING

Finish each exercise session, however short, with a period of relaxation. The Pose of Tranquillity (*page 51*) is a favourite of yoga practitioners, and many classes end with this relaxation technique. Try not to eat for at least half-an-hour after exercising. You may take a bath or shower after about 15 minutes.

GENERAL CAUTIONS

Before starting this or any other exercise programme, *check with your doctor* and obtain his or her permission.

If you suffer from an ear or eye condition, or have an eye disorder such as a detached retina, *omit* the inverted postures such as the Half and Full Shoulderstand (*pages 62 and 63*). If you suffer from epilepsy, *avoid* the Cat Stretch series (*pages 68–70*) and rapid breathing such as the Cleansing Breath (Dynamic) described in Chapter 7.

Avoid inverted postures and rapid abdominal breathing if you have hypertension (high blood pressure). If you have heart disease, *avoid* inverted postures and the Half Locust (*page 58*) and The Bow (*page 59*).

Omit practice of the inverted postures during the monthly menstrual period. At this time, however, the Spread Leg Stretch (*page 54*), the Knee and Thigh Stretch (*page 39*) and the Pelvic Stretch (*page 56*) may be beneficial.

If you have a hernia, *avoid* The Camel (*page 56*), The Cobra (*page 57*), the Half Locust (*page 58*) and The Bow (*page 59*). *Omit* The Plough (*page 54*) if you suffer from neck pain or have spinal disc problems, and *avoid* the Fish Posture (*page 49*) and The Camel (*page 56*) if you have a thyroid gland problem or neck pain.

If you have varicose veins *omit* the Sun Salutations (*pages 65–68*). If you have venous blood clots, *avoid* sitting for any length of time in the folded-legs positions (the Perfect Posture, *page 37*, for example).

Pregnant women and those who have recently given birth are referred to my book entitled *Easy Pregnancy with Yoga* for postures contraindicated pre- and post-natally. Those with back problems will benefit from reading my book entitled *The Yoga Back Book* (*see the Bibliography for details of both titles*).

Contraindications for specific exercises are given in Chapter 6.

CHAPTER FIVE ⟶

WARMING UP AND COOLING DOWN

Warm-ups are a very important part of any exercise programme. They help reduce stiffness, increase body temperature and improve lymph and blood circulation. They also help to prevent muscular pulls and strains once the actual exercises are in progress.

Many of the warm-ups to follow can be incorporated into your daily schedule to prevent an accumulation of tension. By discouraging build-up of tension, you help prevent aches and pain.

WARM-UPS

The Neck

FIGURE-EIGHT EXERCISE

This exercise reduces stiffness and promotes flexibility of the cervical (neck) part of the spine.

1. Sit comfortably. Close your eyes or keep them open. Keep your shoulders, arms and hands relaxed. Breathe regularly throughout the exercise.
2. Imagine a large figure-eight lying on its side in front of you. Starting at the middle, trace its outline with your nose or mouth a few times in one direction.

3. Pause briefly, then trace the outline of the figure-eight a few times in the other direction. Rest.

EAR-TO-SHOULDER

The ear-to-shoulder exercise tones and firms the muscles running from below the ears, across the neck and into the chest. It helps maintain the contour of the neck by exercising the platysma – a broad, flat layer of muscle extending from both sides of the neck to the jaws. This exercise also improves the circulation to the face and reduces the build-up of tension in the neck.

1. Sit comfortably. Hold your spine naturally erect. Keep your jaws, shoulders, arms and hands relaxed. Close your eyes or leave them open. Breathe regularly throughout the exercise.
2. Tilt your head sideways, as if to touch your shoulder with your ear. Bring your head upright.
3. Tilt your head towards the opposite shoulder. Bring your head upright.
4. Repeat the entire process a few times in smooth succession. Rest.

Shoulders

ROTATING

Rotating the shoulders enhances the effects of the neck exercises. It prevents tension from building up in the shoulders and upper back and reduces stiffness in the shoulder joints. It also improves circulation in the shoulders, upper back and neck.

1. Sit comfortably. Hold your spine naturally erect. Keep your jaws, arms and hands relaxed. Close your eyes or keep them open. Breathe regularly throughout the exercise.
2. Pull your shoulders downwards and backwards, squeezing your shoulderblades together.
3. Bring them forwards and upwards, then backwards and downwards to complete one rotation.
4. Do a few more shoulder rotations, *slowly, smoothly and with awareness*, then repeat the rotations several times in the opposite direction. Rest.

Note. You may practise rotating your shoulders while standing.

Hips and Legs

THE BUTTERFLY

The Butterfly reduces stiffness in the ankle, knee and hip joints. It stretches and tones the adductor muscles running along the inner thighs. It improves circulation in the pelvic area.

1. Sit comfortably. Hold your spine naturally erect. Relax your jaws and shoulders. Breathe regularly throughout the exercise.
2. Fold your legs, one at a time, bringing the soles of your feet together. Clasp your hands around your feet and bring your feet comfortably close to your body.
3. Alternately lower and raise your knees, like a butterfly flapping its wings. Do this as many times as you wish, in smooth succession.
4. Carefully unfold your legs and stretch them out, one at a time. Rest.

The Butterfly

THE LYING TWIST

This warm-up firms and strengths the oblique and transverse abdominal muscles (part of the 'abdominal corset') and those of the lower back. It helps keep the waistline trim and promotes a healthy pelvis.

1. Lie on your back, with your arms sideways at shoulder level. Breathe regularly.
2. Bend your legs, one at a time, until the soles of your feet are flat on the mat.
3. Bring your knees towards your chest.
4. Keeping your shoulders and arms in firm contact with the mat, slowly, smoothly and carefully tilt your knees to one side as you exhale (*page 35*). You may keep your head still or turn it to the side opposite your knees.
5. Inhale and bring your knees back to the upright position, as in step 3.

The Lying Twist

6. Exhale and tilt your knees to the opposite side, keeping your head still or turning it opposite to your knees.
7. Repeat the side-to-side tilting of your knees several times in slow, smooth succession.
8. Stretch out and rest.

Ankles

ROTATING
Rotating your ankles improves the circulation to your feet and legs and improves the flexibility of your ankle joints.

1. Sit where you can move your feet freely. Maintain good posture. Breathe regularly throughout the exercise.
2. Rotate your ankles in slow, smooth circles a few times.
3. Repeat the rotations in the opposite direction.

Hands

The following exercises keep your wrist and fingers flexible. They improve coordination and circulation, and strengthen your fingers

and hands. They may also be of help in relieving arthritic pain.

Exercise 1. Breathing regularly, vigorously rub your hands together, several times, to warm them.
Exercise 2. Briskly shake your hands, several times, as if trying to rid them of drops of water. Keep breathing regularly.
Exercise 3. Rotate your wrists, several times in slow, smooth succession (visualize drawing circles with your fingers). Breathe regularly throughout the exercise.

Whole body

ROCK-AND-ROLL
This exercise conditions the back and abdominal muscles, and helps to loosen tight hamstrings (muscles at the back of the legs). These affect the tilt of the pelvis and, therefore, posture. In addition, when you practise the Rock-and-Roll, you press on 64 traditional acupuncture points.

1. Sit on your mat. Bend your legs and rest the soles of your feet flat on the mat, comfortably close to your bottom.
2. Pass your arms under your knees and hug your thighs. Tilt your head down and tuck in your chin. Make your back as rounded as you can. Breathe regularly throughout the exercise.
3. Inhaling, kick backwards to help you roll onto your back (*page 36*).
4. Exhaling, kick forwards and come again into a sitting position. *Be careful* not to land heavily onto your feet as you may jar your spine. Simply touch the mat lightly with your feet or toes.
5. Repeat steps 3 and 4 several times in smooth succession, synchronizing your

Rock–and–Roll

breathing with the rock-and-roll movements. Rest.

Note. Other warm-ups to try are the Sun Salutations (*pages 65–68*) and the Cat Stretch series (*pages 68–70*).

COOLING DOWN

It is important to cool down after exercising. Cooling down affords the chance for static muscle stretching, which enhances flexibility. It provides an activity for the cardiovascular (heart and blood vessels) system to return to normal in a gradual way. It helps prevent problems related to a sudden drop in blood pressure – such as dizziness and fainting – which can occur if exercise is stopped abruptly.

All the warm-up exercises in this chapter, *except* the Rock-and-Roll (*left*) may be done as cool-down exercises. You may also practise the Stick Posture (*page 48*) and even the Sun Salutations (*pages 65–68*) if you do them slowly enough.

You may finish your exercise session, as many yoga students do, with the Pose of Tranquillity (*page 51*).

CHAPTER SIX

THERAPEUTIC EXERCISES

In chapter 2, I explained in general terms how the regular practice of yoga techniques works to maintain good health and to restore it when it has been damaged. In this chapter I explain the specific benefits of each exercise described.

The therapeutic exercises will be divided into sitting, standing, lying, forwards bending, backwards bending, sideways stretching and twisting, inverted and 'series' postures.

SITTING POSTURES

THE BUTTERFLY
This posture (*page 34*) was described in Chapter 5, and is a good preparation for all folded-legs postures.

THE PERFECT POSTURE

Cautions
If you have venous blood clots, omit from your exercise programme the Perfect Posture and similar folded-legs postures.

Benefits
The Perfect Posture (and similar sitting positions) helps tone various nerve centres in the pelvic region.

By resting the body solidly on the ground, in a triangle formed by the hips and thighs, with the spine in good perpendicular alignment, you acquire a sense of mind-body balance. The Perfect Posture (and sitting positions like it) also helps you to develop the ability to remain quietly seated for periods of meditation and for breathing exercises.

Because of the firm, stable base provided by this and similar positions, the spine is held naturally erect, allowing all internal organs to fall naturally into their intended positions without being cramped. Blood circulation to all structures is facilitated, leading to an improvement in their functioning. Breathing becomes easier and more efficient, and all

Perfect Posture

tissues receive a better supply of oxygen. Because of improved oxygenation, thinking becomes clearer and emotions more stable.

How to Do It
1. Sit comfortably upright, with your legs stretched out in front. Bend your right leg and place the sole of your foot against your left thigh, as far up as possible.
2. Bend your left leg and carefully place your foot in the crease formed by the right thigh and calf (*page 37*).
3. Rest your hands on your knees or upturned in your lap.
4. After a while, change the position of your legs so that your right leg is uppermost.

Note. If your knees do not immediately come close to or touch the mat, do not despair. They will when, with regular exercise, your joints become more flexible and your ligaments more elastic.

You may try sitting on a small pillow or cushion about 15 centimetres (6 inches) thick. This will raise your body and, at the same time, allow your knees to come nearer the mat.

JAPANESE SITTING POSITION

Cautions
Avoid using the Japanese Sitting Position if you have venous blood clots or varicose veins.

Benefits
As with other yoga seated postures, the Japanese Sitting Position provides a stable base and encourages good posture. With the spine in good alignment, internal organs will not be cramped and can therefore function properly.

The Japanese Sitting Position is a good way to sit following a large meal as it facilitates digestion (for the reasons stated above).

Japanese Sitting Position

How to Do It
1. Kneel with your legs together and your body upright but not rigid. Point your feet straight backwards.
2. Lower your body until you are sitting on your heels (use your hands to help if necessary).
3. Rest your hands on your thighs or knees (*above*).
4. Sit in this position for as long as you are comfortable in it. Breathe regularly.

SQUATTING POSTURE

Cautions
If you have varicose veins, practise a dynamic version of this posture rather than trying to maintain it for any length of time. To do this, alternate between going into the position and, without staying in it, come up again, as many times as you wish. Be sure, however, to *check first with your doctor* to make sure that no blood clots have formed in your veins.

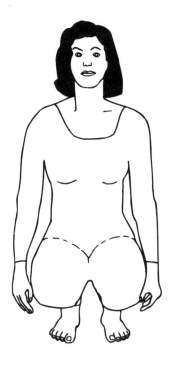

Squatting Posture

Benefits
The Squatting Posture, practised regularly and incorporated into daily activities, is perhaps unsurpassed for helping keep the spine healthy and preventing various back problems.

This posture is also good for strengthening your ankle joints and keeping your knee and hip joints flexible. It is useful, too, for counteracting constipation.

How to Do It
1. Stand with your legs comfortably apart and your arms at your sides. Breathe regularly.
2. Inhale and raise your arms to shoulder level, at the same time rising onto your toes. (If you have difficulty maintaining balance, hold on to a stable prop.)
3. Exhale and slowly lower your arms as well as your body, as if to sit on your heels (*above*).
4. Hold the position as long as you wish or

can with absolute comfort. Keep breathing regularly.
5. Resume your standing position. Sit or lie down and rest.

KNEE AND THIGH STRETCH

Benefits
Practised regularly, the Knee and Thigh Stretch promotes good blood circulation in the pelvis and abdomen. It helps keep the prostate gland, kidneys, bladder and other urinary structures healthy. (Urinary-tract diseases are also said to be rarely found among Indian cobblers who habitually sit in this position.)

How to Do It
1. Sit upright with your legs stretched out in front. Breathe regularly.
2. Fold one leg, and place the heel of your foot as close to your pubic area as you can without straining.
3. Fold your other leg in the same manner, bringing the soles of your feet together.
4. Clasp your hands around your feet and ease your knees towards the mat. You will feel your inner thighs stretch (*below*).

Knee and Thigh Stretch

5. You may keep your hands around your feet as you maintain the thigh stretch, or, alternately, rest your hands (or arms) on your knees to help keep them down.

6. Hold this position for a few seconds to begin with; longer as you become more limber. Maintain good posture and breathe regularly.

7. To come out of the position, rock backwards slightly, put your hands on the mat beside your hips and stretch out your legs, one at a time. Rest.

Note. The Butterfly (*page 34*) is a good preparation for this posture.

MOUNTAIN POSTURE

Benefits
The Mountain Posture tones the pelvic, back and abdominal muscles, and

Mountain Posture

discourages fat deposits around the waist and abdomen. It improves muscular support of the viscera (internal organs).

This posture also tones the chest and arm muscles and helps to improve breathing – through which body cells receive oxygen. In addition, it promotes good circulation.

How to Do It
1. Sit tall in any comfortable folded-legs position, such as the Perfect Posture (*page 37*). Breathe regularly.
2. Inhale and stretch your arms overhead; keep them close to your ears. Press your palms together if you can (*below, left*).
3. Hold this position for as long as you comfortably can, breathing regularly.
4. Exhale and lower your arms; resume your starting position. Rest.

Note. You may practise the Mountain Posture in any comfortable sitting position, such as the Japanese Sitting Position (*page 38*), or while sitting on a bench or stool.

COW HEAD POSTURE

Benefits
This posture is excellent for helping prevent stiffness of the shoulder, arm and leg joints, and thus keeps them flexible. It is also splendid for counteracting the effects of poor postural habits. Cultivating good posture is one positive step to take towards attaining and maintaining good overall health.

How to Do It
1. Sit on your heels in the Japanese Sitting Position (*page 38*). Breathe regularly.
2. Reach over your right shoulder with your right hand. Keep your elbow pointing upwards rather than forwards, and your arm close to your ear.

Cow Head Posture

3. With your left hand, reach behind your back from below, and interlock your fingers with those of your right hand. Maintain a naturally erect posture and breathe regularly throughout the exercise (*above*).

4. Hold this position as long as you comfortably can. *Do not* hold your breath.

5. Resume your starting position. Shrug your shoulders a few times or rotate them if you wish. Rest briefly.

6. Repeat steps 2 to 5, changing the position of your arms and hands (substitute the word 'left' for 'right' and vice versa in the instructions).

Note. You can practise the Cow Head Posture while standing, sitting on a stool or bench, or in a folded-legs position. If you are unable to interlock your fingers as described in step 3, use a scarf, belt or other suitable item as an extension to your arms. Toss one end over your shoulder and reach behind and below to grasp the other end. Pull upwards with your upper hand and downwards with your lower.

ANGLE BALANCE

Benefits
The Angle Balance is excellent for toning and strengthening the abdominal muscles, and thus for providing effective support for abdominal structures such as the stomach and intestines. Strong abdominal muscles are also imperative for a healthy back. The Angle Balance is, moreover, a superb exercise for helping to prevent constipation.

Because it is a balancing exercise, it develops concentration and temporarily diverts attention from various environmental stimuli, some of which may be disturbing. This process has a calming effect on the system, which is beneficial to people suffering from gastritis, peptic ulcers and irritable bowel syndrome.

How to Do It
1. Sit with your legs bent and the soles of your feet flat on the mat. Breathe regularly.

2. Tilt backwards so that you balance on your bottom; bring your legs closer to your body and lift your feet off the mat (use your hands to help, if necessary). Keep breathing regularly and give full attention to what you are doing; it will help you to maintain balance.

3. Stretch out your arms so that they are parallel to the mat.

4. Begin to straighten your legs but do not strain. As you straighten your legs you will need to adjust your degree of tilt to maintain balance (*overleaf*).

5. Hold the completed position for a few seconds to begin with, breathing regularly. As you become more practised, hold the position longer.

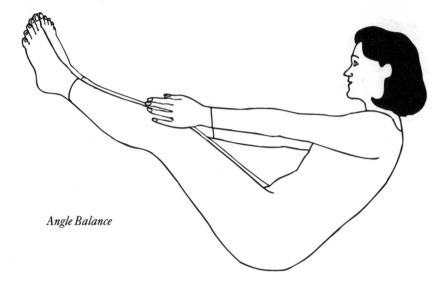

Angle Balance

6. Slowly and carefully return to your starting position.
7. Sit or lie down and rest.

THE FLOWER

Benefits
The flower is an excellent exercise for improving blood circulation to your hands and fingernails. It helps keep your fingers supple and young looking. It helps prevent tension from building up in your hands.

How to Do It
1. Sit naturally upright on your mat. (You may also practise the exercise sitting on a

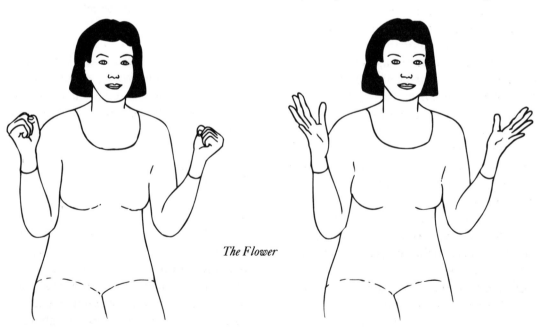

The Flower

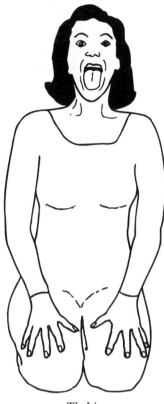

The Lion

chair, standing or lying.) Breathe regularly.
2. Hold your hands, made into tight fists, in front of you (do not simultaneously clench your teeth; keep your jaws relaxed and breathe regularly). (*Page 42*).
3. Slowly, and with resistance, open your hands. Think of them as tightly-closed, sleeping buds opening up unwillingly to the rays of the morning sun.
4. When your hands are fully open, give your fingers a final stretch until they arch backward (*page 42*). Stretch your arms sideways (if circumstances permit) as far as they will go, and hold the open-arms position for a few seconds.
5. Relax your arms and hands.

THE LION

Benefits
This exercise tones your facial muscles and thus improves your appearance. It helps reduce the build-up of tension in your tongue, jaws, lips, throat and facial muscles. It brings a rich supply of blood to the throat, so if you feel a sore throat threatening, practising The Lion may help prevent it from developing. It is also useful in improving the quality of the voice.

How to Do It
1. Sit on your heels in the Japanese Sitting Position (*page 38*). Rest your palms on your thighs or knees. (You may also practise The Lion in any other comfortable position.)
2. Inhale. *Exhale* slowly and at the same time open your eyes and mouth as widely as possible. Very slowly stick out your tongue as far as it will go without straining. Feel the muscles of your face and throat become taut. Stiffen your arms and spread out your fingers. The idea is to look as fierce as possible (*left*).
3. Hold the position as long as your exhalation lasts with absolute comfort, then slowly relax your tongue, face, arms and hands. Continue breathing regularly as you rest. Visualize all tension draining away from your face and throat.

Standing Postures

PRAYER POSE

Benefits
When you are in this position your chest is full and round, facilitating deep breathing. The abdomen is given its greatest length and pelvic organs are relieved of pressure from above.

The Prayer Pose encourages good spinal

Prayer Pose

The Tree

alignment; helps to correct postural defects; encourages muscular coordination and balance; facilitates the distribution of the body's weight along the 132 articulations of the spinal column, and so helps to prevent fatigue. (An articulation is a place of union between two bones.) It also promotes physical and mental steadiness.

How to Do It
1. Stand as tall as you can without rising onto your toes, with your feet close together and parallel to each other.
2. Check that your head is well poised; that your chin is neither tucked down nor jutting forwards.
3. Keep your shoulderblades flat.

4. Tilt your pelvis to prevent any exaggeration of the spinal curve at the small of your back (the lumbar arch).
5. Keep your knees straight but not stiff; keep your legs together.
6. Bring your hands together in front of your breastbone (in prayer position). Relax your facial muscles and jaws; breathe regularly (*above, left*). Focus your attention on an object in front of you or on your breathing, to help keep you steady.
7. Maintain this position for a minute or two to begin with; longer as you become more comfortable with it.

THE TREE

Benefits
This is an excellent posture for cultivating nerve-muscle coordination, balance, alertness and nerve control.

How to Do It
1. Stand tall, with your feet close together and parallel to each other. Establish good posture (*see page 44*) and breathe regularly. Keep your eyes open.
2. Lift one leg and, with the help of your hands, place the sole of your foot against the inner aspect of your opposite thigh. Bring your hands together in front of your breastbone (*page 44*).
3. Maintain this position for as long as you comfortably can, breathing regularly and focusing your attention on the breathing process.
4. When you are ready to come out of the position, straighten your bent leg and resume your starting position. Relax your hands at your sides.
5. Repeat the exercise, balancing this time on your other foot.

BALANCE POSTURE

Benefits
The Balance Posture develops and enhances concentration, nerve-muscle coordination and alertness. It also conditions the quadriceps muscles of the thighs, which help to straighten the knees.

How to Do It
1. Stand tall, with your feet comfortably, but not too far, apart, and your body weight equally distributed. Breathe regularly.
2. Shift your weight onto your right foot. Focus attention on your breathing to help you to keep your balance.

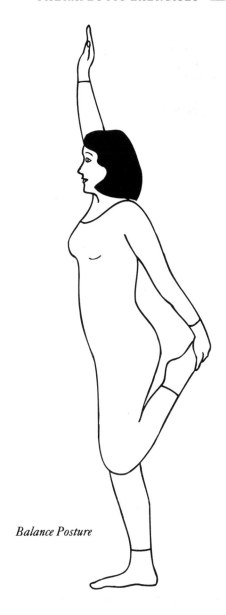

Balance Posture

3. Bend your left leg and point your foot backwards; grasp your foot with your left hand and bring it as close to your buttock as you can with absolute comfort.
4. Keep breathing regularly and raise your right arm upwards to help you to maintain balance (*above, right*).
5. Hold the position as long as you wish or can, remembering to breathe regularly and to

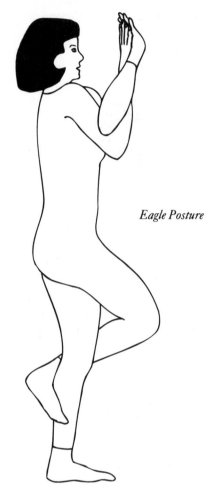

Eagle Posture

any tendency to stiffness and limited functioning. Since it is a balancing exercise, the Eagle Posture also helps to develop and enhance concentration, nerve-muscle coordination and alertness.

How to Do It
1. Stand naturally erect. Relax your arms at your sides. Keep your eyes open and breathe regularly throughout the exercise.
2. Slowly lift your *right* leg. Do so with awareness so that you maintain your balance.
3. Cross your right leg over your left and hook your toes around your left lower leg. Adjust your posture to facilitate these movements.
4. When your stance is secure, try to straighten your body without putting unnecessary pressure on your left leg.
5. Now bend your *right* arm and position it in front of you.
6. Do the same with your left arm, placing it within your bent right arm and rotating your wrists until your palms are together (*left*).
7. Hold this position as long as you comfortably can. If you focus attention on your regular breathing it will help you maintain balance.
8. When you are ready to come out of the position, do so slowly and with awareness. Rest.
9. Repeat steps 2 to 8, changing leg and arms (substitute the word 'left' for 'right' and vice versa).

CHEST EXPANDER

Benefits
This is a superb exercise for reducing the build-up of tension in your shoulders and upper back. Practise it periodically throughout your work day if you spend a lot of time sitting at a desk, or engaged in activities that require you to bend forwards. The Chest Expander also helps to improve posture and

focus attention on the flow of your breath to help keep you steady.
6. Slowly resume your starting position. Rest briefly.
7. Repeat steps 2 to 6, balancing on the left foot this time. Relax at the end of the exercise.

EAGLE POSTURE

Benefits
The Eagle Posture provides an opportunity to exercise all the joints of your arms and legs. This promotes suppleness and elasticity of these joints, thus counteracting

Chest Expander

facilitates deep breathing (through which every cell of your body receives oxygen).

How to Do It
1. Stand tall with your feet comfortably apart and your arms at your sides. Breathe regularly. (You may also do this exercise in any comfortable sitting position.)
2. Inhale and raise your arms sideways to shoulder level; turn your palms downwards.
3. Exhale and lower your arms. Swing them behind you and interlace the fingers of one hand with those of the other. Keep breathing regularly.

4. With fingers still interlaced, raise your arms upwards to their comfortable limit; keep them straight (*left*).
5. Hold this position for as long as you comfortably can. *Do not* hold your breath.
6. Slowly lower your arms, unlock your fingers and relax. You may shrug or rotate your shoulders a few times. Rest.

ABDOMINAL LIFT

Cautions
Do not practise this exercise if you have high blood pressure, an ulcer of the stomach or intestine (peptic ulcer), a heart problem or a hernia. Omit it also during menstruation or pregnancy. In any case, *check with your doctor* before attempting this posture. Always practise this exercise on an empty or near-empty stomach; never immediately after eating.

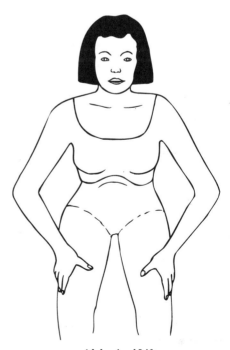

Abdominal Lift

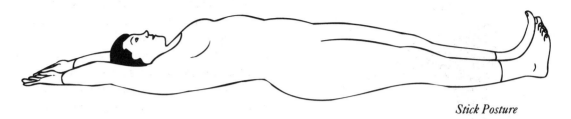

Stick Posture

Benefits

This is an excellent exercise for toning and firming your abdominal muscles, which support your abdominal organs and other internal structures. Healthy abdominal muscles also play a part in maintaining the health of your back.

This is a superb exercise to practise regularly if you tend to suffer from constipation.

How to Do It

1. Stand with your feet about 25 centimetres (10 inches) apart.
2. Bend your knees and turn them slightly outwards, as if preparing to sit.
3. Place your hands on their respective thighs. Keep your torso as erect as you comfortably can and breathe regularly.
4. *Exhale* and with the air still expelled, briskly *pull in your abdomen*, as if to touch your spine with it, *and also pull it upwards,* towards your ribs (*page 47*).
5. Hold the abdominal contraction until you feel the urge to inhale.
6. Inhale and straighten yourself. Rest briefly, resuming normal breathing.
7. Repeat the exercise once, if you wish. You can also repeat it later.

LYING POSTURES

ROCK-AND-ROLL
This posture (*page 36*) was described in Chapter 5.

STICK POSTURE

Benefits

This posture provides an all-body stretch which helps improve the tone of your skeletal muscles (covering your body's bony framework). It also promotes relaxation, improves your general circulation and discourages a build-up of fatty deposits, especially around the waist.

How to Do It

1. Lie on your back, with your legs together and your arms beside you. You can close your eyes or keep them open. Breathe regularly.
2. On an inhalation, sweep your arms sideways, and then overhead, until they are stretched to full length; bring your palms together if you can. At the same time, stretch your body and legs to their fullest comfortable extent; pull your toes upwards and push your heels down (*above*).
3. Hold this position for several seconds but *do not* hold your breath.
4. Exhale and resume your starting position. Rest.

You may repeat this exercise once now, and again later. You can also do the exercise in a standing position, modifying the instructions accordingly.

Supine Knee Squeeze

SUPINE KNEE SQUEEZE

Benefits
This is an excellent exercise for helping to rid your body of gas. It is also superb for relaxing your back, and acts as a counter-posture to relax the front of your body after doing backwards-bending exercises such as The Cobra (*page 57*).

How to Do It
1. Lie on your back with your legs stretched out in front and your arms beside you. Breathe regularly.
2. Exhale and bring first one bent knee, then the other, towards your abdomen. Hold your knees or lower legs securely in place (*above*).
3. Maintain this position for as long as you are comfortable, breathing regularly.
4. Stretch out one leg at a time and rest.

FISH POSTURE

Cautions
Avoid practice of the Fish Posture if you have an abdominal hernia or neck pain, or if you suffer from vertigo, dizziness or balance disorders. Also *avoid* it during the first three days of menstruation, and *check with your doctor* if you have a thyroid gland problem and are considering practising this posture.

Benefits
The Fish Posture is a splendid exercise for those who suffer from asthma and other respiratory conditions.

Through interal massage and stretching of the mid-trunk, it also contributes to the health of organs within your abdomen and pelvis and is effective against constipation.

How to Do It
1. Lie on your back with your legs stretched out in front and your arms beside you, palms turned down.
2. Bend your arms, push down on your elbows, and raise your chest off the mat as you arch your back.
3. Carefully stretch your neck and ease your head towards your shoulders; rest the top of your head on the mat. Adjust your position so that most of your weight is taken by your bottom and elbows, rather than your head and neck (*below*).
4. Hold this position for a few seconds to

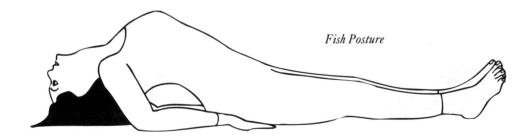

Fish Posture

begin with, breathing slowly and as deeply as possible. Hold the posture longer when you feel more comfortable in it.

5. Slowly and carefully resume your starting position. Rest.

Note. The Supine Knee Squeeze (*page 49*) is a good position in which to relax after practising the Fish Posture.

LEGS UP

Benefits

This exercise is a good way to relieve tired, swollen feet. Also, by helping the return flow of blood from the legs to the heart, and lessening the wear and tear on the valves (which prevent a back-flow of blood) of the large blood vessels, it is wonderful for discouraging the formation or worsening of varicose veins.

The Legs Up exercise is also a good way to promote all-over relaxation if combined with slow rhythmical breathing.

How to Do It

1. Lie near a wall. Rest your legs against the wall so that they form about a 45 degree angle with the mat on which you are lying. Relax your arms at your sides, close your eyes

and breathe slowly and regularly.

2. When you are ready to get up, do so slowly and carefully; bring your knees towards your abdomen, roll onto your side and come into a sitting position.

POSE OF TRANQUILLITY

Benefits

The Pose of Tranquillity is without equal for inducing deep relaxation of nerves and muscles and in helping to eliminate built-up tension. Practised in the evening, it is excellent for promoting sound sleep as it acts as a superb natural tranquillizer. It is a splendid tool for managing stress, and is well worth mastering for use in pain control and dealing with anxiety states.

This posture also helps keep your blood pressure within normal limits and is a useful

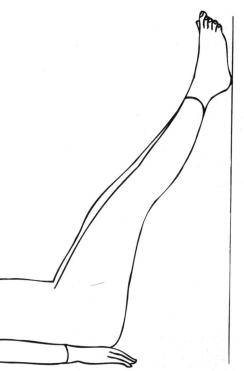

Legs Up

Pose of Tranquillity

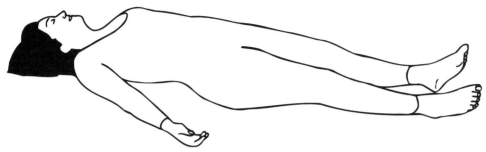

complement to other treatments for those with heart disease. It trains you to conserve energy and contributes to vitality and poise.

How to Do It

1. Lie comfortably in a quiet room. Close your eyes. Unclench your teeth to relax your jaws, and establish slow, regular breathing. Separate your legs to discourage tension from building up in your thighs and hips. Move your arms away from your sides to prevent tension from accumulating in your shoulders. Turn your palms upwards. Position your head for maximum comfort and minimum tension (*above*).

2. Push your heels away from your body, bringing your toes towards you. Maintain this muscular tension for a few seconds. (This will subsequently be referred to as 'hold'.) Now release the tension (subsequently referred to as 'release') and let your legs sink, with their full weight, onto the mat.

3. Squeeze your buttocks together very tightly. Hold. Release.

4. *Exhale* and firmly press the small of your back against the mat. Tighten your abdominal muscles. Hold for as long as your exhalation lasts. Release while inhaling.

5. *Inhale* deeply and squeeze your shoulderblades together. Hold while breathing normally. Release as you exhale.

6. Shrug your shoulders, as if to touch your ears with them. Hold. Release.

7. Carefully tilt your head backwards. Hold. Release.

8. Gently tilt your head forwards, tucking your chin in. Hold. Release.

9. Raise your eyebrows, squeezing your forehead to form horizontal wrinkles. Hold. Release.

10. Squeeze your eyes tightly shut. Hold. Release.

11. *Exhaling*, open your eyes and mouth; stick your tongue out; stare; tense all facial muscles (*see The Lion, page 43*). Hold. Release. Again, close your eyes.

12. Now shift your attention to your arms and hands. Stiffen them; make tight fists; raise them off the mat. Hold. Release. Again, rest your arms and hands beside you, as in step 1.

13. Turn your thoughts to your breathing now. Each time you exhale, let yourself sink more fully into your mat, increasingly relaxed. Each time you inhale, visualize an intake of positive forces, such as peace and health. Spend several minutes on this part of the exercise.

14. When you are ready to finish, bring yourself out of the deeply relaxed state you will have entered in a gradual way. Stretch your limbs leisurely and do any other gentle movements you wish. Never get up suddenly.

The Crocodile

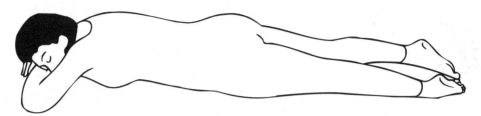

Note. This is a basic technique. There are many variations and only practice will teach you the precise version that is right for *you*.

You may practise the Pose of Tranquillity in bed if you are unwell, or in an easy chair. Modify the exercise instructions accordingly.

THE CROCODILE

Benefits
The same as for the Pose of Tranquillity (*page 51*).

How to Do It
1. Lie on your abdomen, with your legs fully stretched out and comfortably separated. (You may place a thin pillow or cushion under your hips.)
2. Fold your arms and rest your head on them, as depicted *above*. Close your eyes. Breathe regularly.
3. Mentally go over your body from your toes to your head, concentrating on one part at a time, giving each part silent suggestion to let go of tension and to relax completely. Include the feet, legs, hips, upper back, abdomen, chest, arms and hands, neck, head and facial muscles.
4. If your thoughts stray, gently guide them back and continue the exercise.
5. Finish with several minutes of slow rhythmical breathing, letting your body sink more fully onto your mat with each exhalation.
6. Roll onto your side and use your hands to help you up.

FORWARDS BENDING POSTURES

BACK-STRETCHING POSTURE

Cautions
Avoid practising this posture if you suffer from a disease of the liver, spleen or appendix, or if you have a hernia. It should also be omitted if you are pregnant.

Benefits
The Back-stretching Posture is excellent for providing a gentle traction on the spine, which releases pressure on spinal nerves. It stretches your back muscles therapeutically, helping to keep them in peak condition as effective spinal supports.

This posture also helps to keep your hip and shoulder joints flexible; and your elbow joints, if these are bent during the exercise. Ankle joints benefit from practising a variation of this exercise in which the toes point upwards and the big toes are held.

How to Do It
1. Sit naturally erect on your mat, with your legs together, stretched out in front and in firm contact with the mat. Breathe regularly.
2. Inhale and raise your hands overhead.
3. Exhaling, bend forwards at your hip joints rather than at your waist; keep your torso erect. Reach for your feet.
4. When you have reached your comfortable limit, hold on to a convenient part of your

Back-stretching Posture

legs, or to your ankles or feet (*above*). If you
can, hold on to your big toes. Lower your
head and relax in the position.

5. Hold the posture for as long as you are
comfortable in it. Breathe regularly.

6. Come out of the position slowly in reverse,
synchronizing breathing with movement.

7. Lie down and rest.

The Cobra (*page 57*) is a good exercise to
practise following the Back-stretching
Posture.

STAR POSTURE

Benefits

This is a very good exercise for toning and
firming your inner thigh muscles and your
perineum (the lowest part of your torso), and
for improving circulation to your pelvis.

It helps keep your hip, knee and ankle
joints, as well as your spine flexible, and
prevents backache and back fatigue.

How to Do It

1. Sit comfortably erect, with your legs
stretched out in front. Breathe regularly.

2. Bend one leg and place the sole of your
foot flat on the mat, opposite the knee of
your outstretched leg. Maintain this distance
between foot and body when you perform
the exercise.

3. Bend your outstretched leg. Place the
soles of your feet together, allowing your
knees to fall towards the mat.

Star Posture

4. Clasp your hands around your feet
without shifting their position.

5. Exhaling, bend forwards slowly and with
control, bringing your face towards your feet.
Once you have reached your comfortable
limit, relax and breathe regularly (*above*).

6. Hold the position for as long as you are
comfortable in it.

7. Slowly resume your starting position,
synchronizing movement with breathing.

8. Lie down and rest.

SPREAD LEG STRETCH

Benefits

The Spread Leg Stretch brings a good
supply of blood to your perineal area (the
lowest part of your torso), and thus
contributes to the health of your pelvis. It
tones and firms your inner thigh muscles and
improves circulation in your legs. It also
helps to keep your spine flexible and relieves
pressure on spinal nerves.

Diligent practice of this exercise will
contribute to relief from menstrual cramps
and backache.

How to Do It

1. Sit naturally upright on your mat, with
your legs spread as far apart as is comfortable.

Spread Leg Stretch

Place your hands on your legs, with your palms turned downwards.

2. Exhale and bend forwards, at your hip joints rather than at your waist; keep your torso erect. Slide your hands downwards as if to touch your feet (*above*).

3. When you can bend no further, hold the position as long as you are comfortable in it. Keep breathing regularly.

4. Inhale and slowly resume your starting position. Rest.

THE PLOUGH

Cautions

Do not practise The Plough during the first few days of menstruation or the last five or six months of pregnancy. *Avoid* it also if you have a uterine prolapse or a hernia, or if you suffer from neck pain or spinal disc problems.

In any event, *check with your doctor* before practising The Plough. If you do practise the exercise, be especially careful not to exert unnecessary pressure on your neck. *Do not* let your buttocks go beyond your shoulders, as this can place too much strain on your neck.

Benefits

Studies in India indicate that regular practice of The Plough can lengthen the spine, in some cases by nearly 15 per cent. When this occurs, the vertebral foramina (openings), through which the spinal nerves pass, are enlarged, and pressure on these nerves is eased. (Faulty postures during day-to-day activities result in such pressure.) This improves the circulation in your spinal cord (which is an extension of your brain), and thus also the functioning of internal organs supplied by these nerves.

The Plough is effective in preventing an accumulation of toxic substances in the body. The contraction of the abdominal muscles and the hips-high, head-low position help drain internal structures and strengthen them. Wastes are effectively eliminated and

The Plough

your body becomes healthier and your mind clearer.

How to Do It

1. Lie on your back, with your arms stretched out at your sides and the palms of your hands turned downwards. Breathe regularly.
2. Bring your knees to your chest, then straighten your legs so that your feet point upwards. (Do not raise both legs upwards at the same time from a lying position, as you may hurt your back.)
3. On an exhalation, kick backwards with both feet at once until your hips are raised. Push your feet towards the mat behind your head. Keep your legs straight and together if possible (*page 54*).
4. Hold the completed position for as long as you can with absolute comfort. Breathe regularly.
5. To resume your starting position, *slowly, smoothly and carefully* roll your spine onto the mat; bend your legs and stretch them out. Rest.

Note. Do not be discouraged if your toes do not immediately touch the mat. They will, eventually, as your spine becomes flexible. In the meantime, you can try putting a few cushions behind you so that your feet can touch something. This will serve as a guide to your progress.

POSE OF A CHILD

Benefits

This posture, regularly practised, helps keep your spine flexible. As you breathe rhythmically while in this position, your internal organs receive a gentle, therapeutic massage which promotes circulation and facilitates elimination.

The Pose of a Child is a restful position in which to relax.

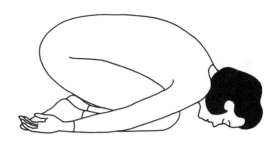

Pose of a Child

How to Do It

1. Sit in the Japanese Sitting Position (*page 38*). Breathe regularly.
2. Bend forwards slowly, resting your forehead on the mat or turning your face to the side. Relax your arms and hands beside you (*above*).
3. Stay in this position for as long as you feel comfortable in it. Keep breathing regularly.
4. Slowly resume your starting position.

Note. If you cannot get your head down onto the mat, place a cushion or pillow in front of you and rest your forehead or cheek on it.

TRIANGLE POSTURE

Benefits

For suppleness and elasticity, the Triangle Posture provides therapeutic stretching of various ordinarily under-exercised muscles.

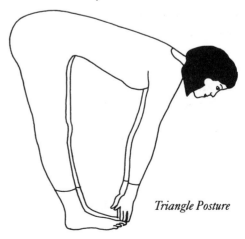

Triangle Posture

It tones the muscles of your back and abdomen and improves muscular support for the organs within your abdomen and pelvis. It offers gentle, effective stretching for the muscles of your legs and arms.

How to Do It
1. Stand erect, with your feet together and your arms at your sides. Breathe regularly.
2. Exhaling, bend forwards at your hips rather than at your waist. Keep your upper body and legs straight.
3. Try to touch your toes with your fingertips. Do not lower your head; keep it aligned with your back (*page 55*).
4. Hold the position for as long as you comfortably can, breathing regularly.
5. Inhale and resume your starting position.

BACKWARDS BENDING POSTURES

PELVIC STRETCH

Benefits
The Pelvic Stretch gives a therapeutic stretch to your groin, and improves circulation in the entire pelvic region. This benefits all pelvic structures.

How to Do It
1. Sit on your heels in the Japanese Sitting Position (*page 38*).
2. Put your hands on the mat behind your feet, with your fingers pointing away from you. Breathe regularly.
3. Inhaling, carefully tilt your head slightly backwards. Press on your palms and raise your bottom off your heels, as high as you comfortably can (*above, right*).
4. Maintain this position for as long as is comfortable, breathing regularly.
5. Slowly ease yourself back into your starting position.

Pelvic Stretch

Note. A good way to rest following this posture is in the Pose of a Child (*page 55*).

THE CAMEL

Cautions
Avoid this posture if you suffer from neck pain or spinal disc problems, or if you have a hernia.

Benefits
The Camel strengthens your back and keeps your spine flexible. It has a beneficial influence on your endocrine glands (such as

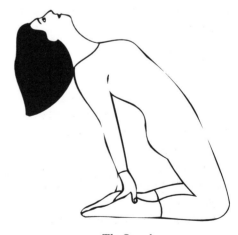

The Camel

the thyroid and the ovaries). It strengthens the urinary and reproductive organs, and helps prevent a build-up of fat around your waist. It also conditions your hip and thigh muscles.

How to Do It

1. Kneel down with your legs together and your toes pointing backwards.
2. Support the small of your back (waist level) with your hands, and *very carefully* tilt your head backwards.
3. *Slowly and carefully* place your right hand on your right heel and your left hand on your left heel. Keep your hips high (*page 56*).
4. Hold this position for as long as you can with absolute comfort, breathing regularly.
5. *Very slowly and carefully* resume your starting position. Rest in the Pose of a Child (*page 55*).

Note. In due course, you may be interested in a more challenging version of this exercise: rest your hands on the mat behind your feet rather than on your heels.

THE COBRA

Cautions

Do not include The Cobra in your exercise programme if you have a hernia or if you are pregnant. (Please note that this exercise is also part of the Sun Salutations, *pages 65–68*.)

Benefits

The Cobra is excellent for promoting and maintaining the elasticity of your spine. It enhances spinal circulation and relieves the pressure on nerves branching off the spine – often a result of bad postural habits. This position also exercises the joints of your shoulders, elbows and wrists and so helps keep them flexible.

As you breathe rhythmically while in this posture, internal structures receive a gentle, yet effective massage, with consequent improvement in function. The Cobra is also useful for counteracting constipation.

How to Do It

1. Lie on your abdomen, with your head turned to the side. Relax your arms and hands beside you. Breathe regularly.
2. Turn your head to the front, resting your forehead on the mat. Place your palms on the mat, directly beneath your shoulders. Keep your arms close to your sides.
3. As you inhale, bend backwards *slowly and carefully*: touch the mat with your nose then your chin, in one smooth movement. Breathe regularly and continue arching the rest of your spine: your upper back then your lower

The Cobra

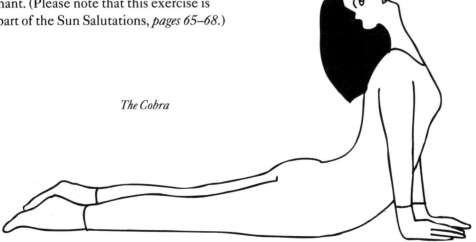

back, in one slow, smooth, graceful movement. Keep your hips in contact with the mat throughout the exercise (*page 57*).

4. When you can arch your back no further, hold the position but *do not hold your breath*. Keep breathing regularly.

5. When you are ready to come out of the position, do so in reverse very *slowly, smoothly and with control*: lower your abdomen to the mat; lower your chest, chin, nose and forehead, in synchronization with regular breathing.

6. Relax your arms and hands beside you. Turn your head to the side. Rest.

HALF LOCUST

Cautions
Avoid the Half Locust if you have a serious heart condition, a hernia or if you are pregnant.

Benefits
Excellent for strengthening your back and your legs, the Half Locust – through gentle, yet effective internal massage – improves the function of structures in your kidney area (kidneys and adrenal glands), and also helps to counteract constipation.

How to Do It
1. Lie on your abdomen, with your chin touching the mat and your legs fairly close together. Straighten your arms and position them, close together, under your body. Make fists and keep your thumbs down. (You may, alternatively, keep your arms alongside your body.) Breathe regularly.

2. Exhale and slowly and carefully raise one still-straight leg as high as you comfortably can. Keep your chin, arms and body pressed to the mat (*below*).

3. Hold the raised-leg posture as long as you comfortably can, breathing regularly.

4. Lower your leg to the mat, slowly and with control. Rest.

5. Repeat the exercise with your other leg.

THE BOW

Cautions
Avoid this exercise if you have a serious heart condition, a hernia or if you are pregnant.

Benefits
The Bow keeps your spine flexible and strengthens your back and abdominal muscles. Through gentle, yet effective massage, it improves the functioning of

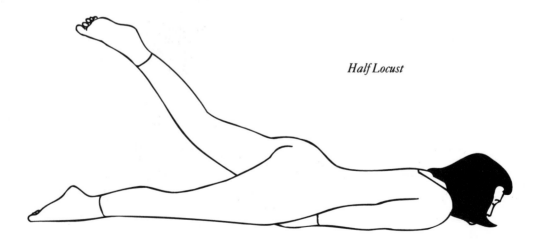

Half Locust

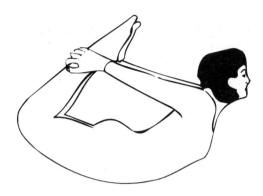

The Bow

organs and glands in the kidney area, as well as those within the abdomen. It helps to counteract constipation, and expands the chest to facilitate deep breathing for the better nourishment of all body tissues.

How to Do It

1. Lie face downwards, with your legs comfortably separated and your arms beside you. Breathe regularly.
2. Bend your knees and bring your feet close to your bottom.
3. *Carefully* tilt your head back; reach for your feet and grasp your ankles. Keep breathing regularly.
4. *Exhaling*, push your feet upwards and away from you. This action will raise your legs and arch your body (*left*).
5. Breathing regularly, hold the position for as long as you comfortably can.
6. Resume your starting position. Push yourself up onto your hands and knees and relax in the Pose of a Child (*page 55*).

SIDEWAYS STRETCHING AND TWISTING POSTURES

THE LYING TWIST
This posture (*page 35*) was described in Chapter 5.

Side Leg Raise

SIDE LEG RAISE

Benefits
This exercise tones the muscles of your inner thighs and improves circulation to your lower pelvis. It also discourages a build-up of fatty deposits around your waist.

How to Do It
1. Lie on your side, supporting your head with your hand. You may bend your lower leg slightly. Rest the palm of your opposite hand on the floor in front of you, for stability.
2. Inhale and slowly raise your upper leg, trying to keep it directly over the lower one, rather than behind or in front of it. Keep your raised leg as straight as you can (*page 59*).
3. Hold this position as long as you comfortably can, breathing regularly.

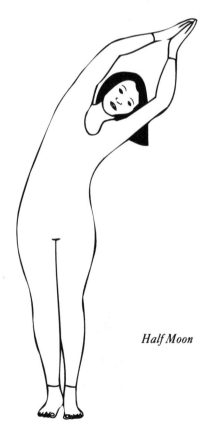

Half Moon

4. Exhale and lower your leg. Rest.
5. Repeat the exercise, lying on the other side this time.

HALF MOON

Benefits
The Half Moon provides sideways (lateral) bending of your torso, thus contributing to the health of your spine. It helps keep your shoulder joints flexible and exercises the midriff to discourage a build-up of fat. It also enhances breathing.

How to Do It
1. Stand naturally erect, with your feet close together, and your body weight equally distributed between them. Relax your arms at your sides. Breathe regularly.
2. Inhale and bring your arms upwards. Press your palms together if you can. Keep your arms alongside your ears.
3. Exhale, and slowly and smoothly bend to one side to form a graceful arch (*left*).
4. Hold this position for as long as you comfortably can, breathing regularly.
5. Inhale and return to the upright position. Exhale and lower your arms.
6. Repeat steps 2 to 5, bending to the other side. Rest.

ANGLE POSTURE

Benefits
Used as a complement to the Triangle Posture (*page 55*), this exercise is excellent for stretching and toning the lateral (side) muscles of your trunk and for discouraging a build-up of fat around your waist. It also improves abdominal and pelvic circulation.

How to Do It
1. Stand erect, with your arms at your sides and your feet about 60 centimetres (24 inches) apart. Breathe regularly.

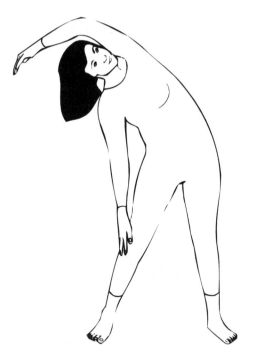

Angle Posture

2. Inhaling, raise your left arm; exhale and bend sideways to the right, sliding your right hand down the side of your right leg. Keep your left arm alongside your ear (*above*).
3. When you can bend no further, hold the position for as long as you are comfortable in it. Continue breathing regularly.
4. Inhale and return to the upright position; exhale and lower your arm.
5. Repeat the sideways bend to the other side (substitute the word 'right' for 'left' and vice versa in the instructions).

SPINAL TWIST

Cautions
Pregnant women will welcome a gentler, more convenient version of this exercise, which is described and illustrated in my *Easy Pregnancy with Yoga* (*see the Bibliography for details*).

Benefits
This is the only yoga exercise that requires maximum torsion (twisting) of the spine; first to one side, then to the other, causing the vertebrae (bones making up the spine) to rotate one over the other and to bend at the same time to the right or left. This spinal action gives a therapeutic massage to nerves branching off the spinal column.

Muscles of the lower back are also stretched and contracted during this exercise. This enhances the blood circulation in the area of your kidneys and

Spinal Twist

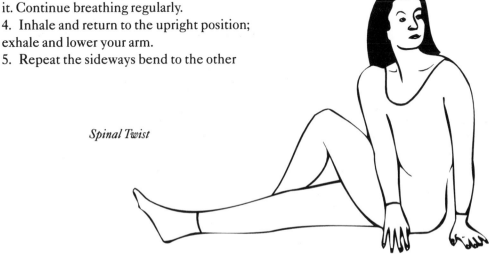

revitalizes your adrenal glands, which lie above your kidneys. To revitalize your adrenal glands is to improve your entire circulatory system and to 'recharge the batteries' of each cell in your body.

How to Do It

1. Sit naturally erect on your mat, with your legs stretched out in front of you. Breathe regularly.
2. Bend your *left* leg at the knee, and place your *left* foot beside the *outer* aspect of your right knee. Keep breathing regularly.
3. On an *exhalation, slowly and smoothly* twist your upper body to the *left*, placing both hands on the mat at your *left* side. Turn your head and look over your *left* shoulder (*page 61*).
4. Hold this position as long as you comfortably can, continuing to breathe regularly.
5. *Slowly and smoothly* untwist and resume your starting position.
6. Repeat steps 2 to 5 in the opposite direction (substitute the word 'right' for 'left' and vice versa in the instructions). Rest.

Note. For an advanced variation of this exercise, fold your lower leg rather than keeping it extended.

INVERTED POSTURES

HALF SHOULDERSTAND

Cautions

Avoid this and other inverted postures if you have an ear or eye disorder, or if you suffer from heart disease, high blood pressure or other circulatory disorders. Do not practise inverted postures during menstruation. In any event, *check with your doctor* before attempting the Half Shoulderstand and other head-low hips-high postures. (*See the general cautions in Chapter 4.*)

Half Shoulderstand

Benefits

By summoning the aid of gravitational forces, this inverted posture greatly benefits the health of your skin and hair. It facilitates circulation to the upper body, enriching tissues such as those of your face and scalp.

The health-giving benefits of this inverted posture are the result of a two-fold mechanism: the stretching and contraction of three muscle groups, namely your back muscles which are stretched; your abdominal muscles which are contracted; and the muscles at the front of your neck which are also contracted.

The organs within your trunk are revitalized, improving blood circulation and the function of the lymphatic, endocrine and nervous systems.

Some also claim that regular practice of this inverted posture (and other similar postures) has helped restore grey hair to its normal colour.

How to Do It

1. Lie on your back on a mat. Bend your knees and rest the soles of your feet flat on

the mat. Keep your arms close to your sides. Breathe regularly throughout the exercise.

2. Bring first one knee, then the other, to your chest.

3. Straighten one leg at a time until your feet point upwards.

4. Kick backwards with both feet at once, until your hips are off the mat. Support your hips with your hands, thumbs in front (*page 62*).

5. Maintain this position for a few seconds to begin with; longer as you become more comfortable with it.

6. To come out of the posture, place your hands on the mat again, close to your body.

7. Keep your head firmly pressed to the mat (perhaps tilting your chin slightly upwards), and *slowly and carefully* lower your torso, from top to bottom, onto the mat. Bend your knees and stretch out your legs, one at a time.

Note. If you are unable to do the Half Shoulderstand but wish to gain some of the benefits of an inverted posture, try the Dog Stretch (*page 64*). *Check with your doctor first.*

FULL SHOULDERSTAND

Cautions
These are the same as for the Half Shoulderstand (*page 62*). *Avoid* the Full Shoulderstand if you suffer from neck pain.

Benefits
The benefits derived from the Full Shoulderstand are the same as those of the Half Shoulderstand. In addition, the gentle pressure exerted on your thyroid gland (in your neck) by the contraction of your neck muscles, as well as an increased blood supply, enhances thyroid gland function. The thyroid gland controls your body's metabolism, so when it is functioning well all cells and tissues benefit.

How to Do It
1. Lie on your back on a mat. Bend your knees and rest the soles of your feet flat on the mat. Keep your arms close to your sides. Breathe regularly throughout the exercise.

2. Bring first one knee, then the other, to your chest.

3. Straighten one leg at a time until your feet point upwards.

4. Kick backwards with both feet at once, until your hips are off the mat. Support your hips with your hands, thumbs in front.

5. Gradually move your hands, one at a time, towards your upper back, until your body is in as vertical a position as you can manage with complete comfort (*below*). Your chin should be in contact with your chest and your body as relaxed as possible.

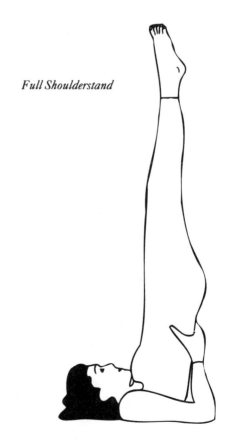

Full Shoulderstand

6. Hold the position for a few seconds to begin with, working up to two or more minutes as you become accustomed to it.

7. To come out of the posture, tilt your feet slightly backwards. Rest your arms beside your body and keep your head pressed to the mat. Slowly lower your hips to the mat. Bend your legs and lower them, one at a time, to the mat. Rest.

MOCK HEADSTAND

Cautions
If you have high blood pressure or neck pain, *check with your doctor* before practising this posture.

Benefits
This exercise brings a fresh supply of blood to the face and scalp, which benefits your skin and hair. It also promotes general relaxation.

How to Do It
1. Sit on your heels, with your toes pointing backwards. Breathe regularly throughout the exercise.

2. Lean forwards and rest your forehead on the mat, close to your knees.

3. *Carefully* raise your bottom from your heels until the top of your head rests on the mat. *Do not exert pressure on your skull.* Hold on to your heels or ankles (*below*).

4. Hold the position for only a few seconds at first, working up to a minute or two as you become more comfortable in it.

5. To come out of the posture ease yourself slowly towards your heels. Keep your head low for a few seconds before gradually sitting upright on your heels. Rest before getting up.

DOG STRETCH

Cautions
Avoid doing the Dog Stretch if you suffer from high blood pressure or have a heart condition. (Please note that this exercise is also part of the Sun Salutations, *pages 65–68*.)

Benefits
This exercise is wonderful for improving the elasticity of your hamstring muscles at the back of your legs. When these muscles shorten, they affect the tilt of your pelvis and may contribute to backache.

The Dog Stretch brings a fresh supply of blood to your upper body and so benefits your skin and scalp. It also promotes general relaxation.

How to Do It
1. Start in an 'all fours' position on your

Mock Headstand

Dog Stretch

hands and knees. Your thighs should be roughly perpendicular to the mat and your arms sloping forwards. Breathe regularly.

2. Tuck your toes forward; rock back slightly; raise your knees and straighten your legs; straighten your arms; look downwards. You are now in a hips-high, head-low position (*page 64*). Aim your heels towards the mat but do not strain the muscles at the back of your legs (hamstrings). Keep breathing regularly.

3. Gently rock forwards before resuming your starting position on hands and knees.

4. Sit on your heels, Japanese-style (*page 38*).

5. Rest in the Pose of a Child (*page 55*) or any other comfortable position.

SERIES POSTURES

SUN SALUTATIONS

Cautions
Avoid these exercises if you have varicose veins, venous blood clots, high blood pressure or a hernia. (*See also cautions for The Cobra (page 57) and the Dog Stretch (page 64).*)

Benefits
The Sun Salutations can be used as warm-up and cool-down exercises, as well as a short, almost complete exercise session when you are pressed for time. They are excellent for promoting overall flexibility, and help to prevent the build-up of fat. A superb tension-reliever, they are also helpful in reducing stress.

Because the Sun Salutations encourage concentration and conscious breathing, they are a splendid set of exercises for promoting a 'fine-tuning-in' to yourself, so you can be more alert to departures from normal functioning. They also improve vitality.

The Sun Salutations are beneficial to the lymphatic system (part of the immune system which protects you from disease). By contracting various muscles, the exercises exert gentle pressure on underlying blood and lymphatic vessels. The non-strenuous stretching action provided by all the different movements temporarily removes 'kinks' from lymphatic vessels and promotes a smoother flow of lymph. (Lymph eliminates waste matter and provides oxygen and other nourishment to the cells of your body.)

How to Do Them
1. Stand tall, with the palms of your hands together in front of your chest (*below*). Breathe regularly.

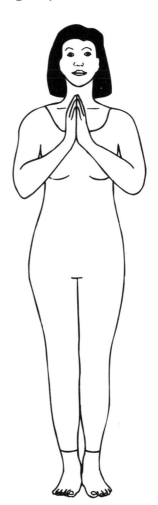

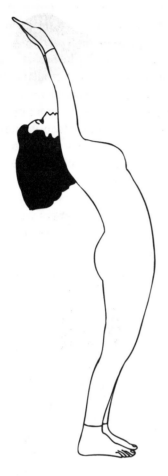

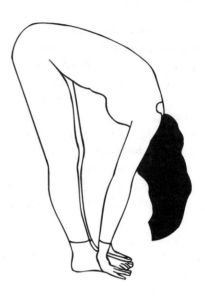

2. *Inhale*, raise your arms and carefully bend backwards to stretch the front of your body. Tighten your buttock muscles to help protect your lower back (*left*).

3. *Exhale* and bend forwards (at your hip joints rather than your waist), and place your hands on the mat beside your feet (*above*). If necessary, bend your knees; as you become more flexible, you will be able to do this step with your knees straight.

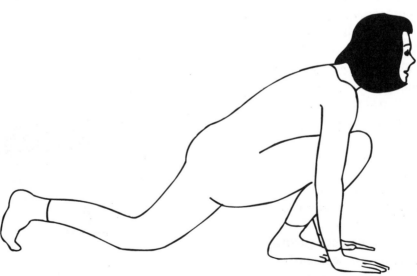

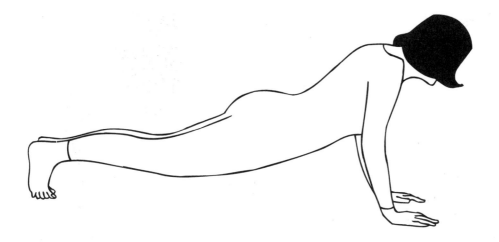

4. *Inhale* and look up. Taking the weight of your body on both hands, step back with your left foot (toes point forwards, *page 66*).

5. Briefly suspending your breath (neither inhaling or exhaling), step backwards with your right foot. The weight of your body is now borne by your hands and feet, and your body is level from the back of your head to your heels (*above*).

6. *Exhale* and lower your knees to the mat. Also lower your chin or forehead (whichever is more comfortable) and chest to the mat (*below*). Relax your feet.

7. *Inhaling,* lower your body to the mat and *slowly and carefully* arch your back. Keep your head up and back, and your hands pressed to the mat (*page 68*). This position is the same as The Cobra (*page 57*).

8. *Exhale* and point your toes forwards; push against the mat with your hands to help raise your hips. Arms are straight (or almost straight), and your head hangs down. Aim your heels towards the mat but *do not strain* (*page 68*). This position is the same as the Dog Stretch (*page 64*).

9. *Inhaling,* look up, rock forwards onto your toes and step between your hands with your *left* foot, *page 66*, (the same foot which you moved backwards in step 4 of these instructions.

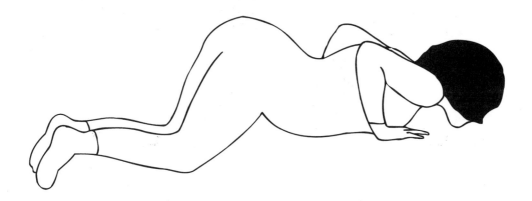

10. *Exhaling,* step between your hands with your right foot and bend forwards (as in step 3 of these instructions, *page 66*).

11. *Inhaling,* come up carefully into a standing position, and move smoothly into the backwards bend described in step 2 of these instructions (*page 66*).

12. *Exhaling,* resume your starting position, as described in step 1 of these instructions (*page 65*). Breathe regularly.

Repeat the sequence (steps 2 to 12) as many times as desired, alternating left foot with right in steps 4 and 9. Rest.

CAT STRETCH SERIES

Cautions

Avoid this series of exercises if you suffer from epilepsy. *Check with your doctor.* If you have just given birth, *omit* step 4 of the exercise instructions.

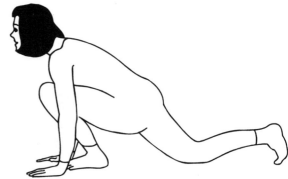

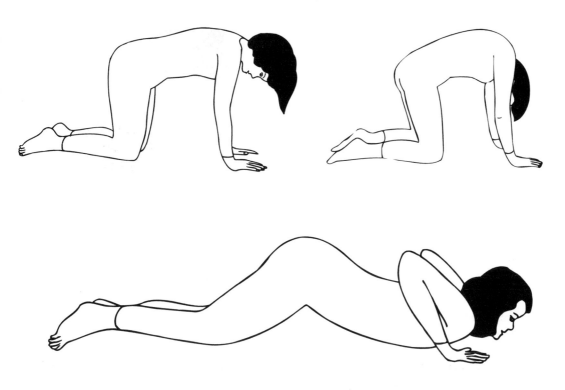

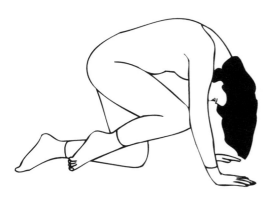

Benefits

The Cat Stretch series helps to keep your spine flexible. It conditions the back muscles which support your spine, and tones and firms your abdominal muscles, which complement your back muscles as spinal supports. It also provides therapeutic stretching of your legs, and improves your general circulation.

How to Do Them

1. Get on your hands and knees in an 'all fours' position (*above, left*).
2. Exhaling, lower your head, arch your shoulders and tuck your hips down so that your entire back is rounded (*above, right*).
3. Inhale and resume your starting position. Exhale.
4. Inhaling, bend your elbows and lower your chest to the mat, taking care not to let your back sag. Keep your head back so that your neck receives a gentle stretch as your chin touches the mat. Let your arms and hands take most of the weight to avoid unnecessary pressure on your back (*above*).
5. Exhale and return to the 'all fours' position. Breathe regularly.
6. Exhaling, lower your head, make your back rounded and bring one knee towards your forehead (*left*).
7. Inhaling, push your bent leg backwards,

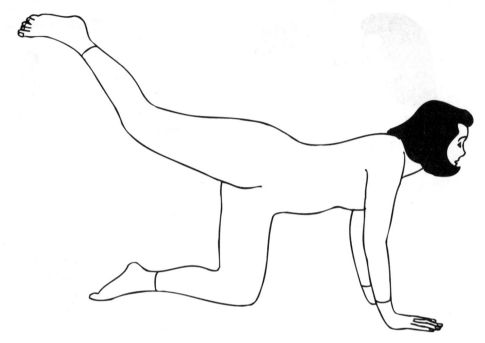

stretching it out fully and lifting it as high as you can with comfort; raise your head (*above*). Take care *not* to accentuate the arch in your lower back as you do this movement.

8. Exhale and lower your knee to the mat.

9. Repeat step 7 with your other leg.

10. Repeat step 8.

11. Lie down and rest, breathing regularly, or rest in the Pose of a Child (*page 55*).

CANDLE CONCENTRATION

Benefits
Candle Concentration promotes relaxation and is a good pre-sleep exercise for those who suffer from insomnia. It improves concentration, facilitates meditation and also helps to improve or correct certain eye weaknesses.

How to Do It
Place a lighted candle at (or slightly below) eye level, on a table, stool or other appropriate place.

1. Sit naturally erect and breathe regularly. Look intently at the candle flame (*page 71*). Blink if necessary.

2. Now close your eyes and retain or recall the image of the flame. Do not be anxious if it disappears. Try to recall the image of the flame and fix your attention on it. Keep breathing regularly.

3. After about two minutes open your eyes. As you become more comfortable with the technique, lengthen practice time to five or ten minutes.

PALMING

Benefits
Palming counteracts eyestrain and reduces the build-up of tension in your face and body. It also promotes concentration.

How to Do It
1. Sit naturally erect at a desk or table, or anywhere else that allows you to rest your elbows comfortably.

Candle concentration

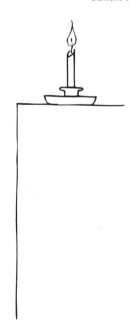

2. Vigorously rub together the palms of your hands to warm them and charge them with natural electricity.

3. Place your palms gently over closed eyes to exclude the light. Rest your fingers lightly on your forehead (*below*). Do not put pressure on your eyeballs. Try to relax your eyelids. Breathe regularly.

4. Stay in this position for a minute or two to begin with; longer as you feel more comfortable with the technique.

5. Keep your eyes closed and repeat steps 2 to 4 if you wish; otherwise proceed to step 6.

6. Separate your fingers and open your eyes to permit a slow reintroduction of light. Relax your arms and hands. Blink your eyes several times if you wish, to finish the exercise.

Palming

CHAPTER SEVEN

BREATHING EXERCISES

An important part of the three-step approach to health, mentioned in Chapter 2, is the practice of special breathing techniques. This chapter offers a selection of breathing exercises which, in yogic parlance, are known collectively as *pranayama*. *Prana* means breath, vitality or energy; *ayama* means stretching or expansion. *Pranayama*, therefore, signifies the extension and control of breath, or voluntarily controlled respiration. It is, in essence, the science of breath, without which life ceases.

BENEFITS

By regularly practising yoga breathing exercises, you increase your potential for truly living rather than merely existing. You learn to become more aware, more alert and more in control of yourself.

Yoga breathing exercises strengthen your respiratory (breathing) system, soothe your nervous system and help to reduce or eliminate various cravings (such as for food, alcohol and nicotine). They also strengthen your immune system. Breathing plays an important role in metabolism – the process by which the body utilizes nutrients. When practised regularly, these exercises therefore have a normalizing effect on both body weight and energy levels.

Because they improve the oxygen supply to all tissues, the exercises also enhance the functioning of all body structures. They help to eliminate irritants that contribute to discomfort and pain, and retrain muscles involved in the breathing process – particularly your diaphragm, which is located between your chest and your abdomen. This improves the venous return of blood to your heart, so that the workload on your heart is reduced and circulation is improved.

By consciously regulating your breath, your mind can be made more at ease and your emotions more stable. When your mind is troubled, both your breathing and heartbeat tend to speed up.

With the exception of the dynamic form of the Cleansing Breath, all the breathing exercises in this chapter may be practised from the beginning of pregnancy, as a preliminary to childbirth preparation.

PREREQUISITES FOR EFFECTIVE BREATHING

1. A naturally erect position of your vertebral column (spine), with your ribcage relaxed to avoid the compression of your lungs and other structures within your chest (such as your heart and large blood vessels).
2. A slow, smooth, deep inhalation; first

using your diaphragm like a suction pump, and then expanding your ribcage with the help of your chest muscles.

3. A slow, steady exhalation; essentially using your diaphragm in reverse as a sort of squeezing pump.

4. A regular breathing rhythm.

5. Unless otherwise specified, breathing through your nostrils, with your mouth closed, so that the air may be warmed, moistened and filtered before it reaches your lungs.

6. A relaxed body (pay special attention to your jaws, face and hands).

PREPARING FOR THE EXERCISES

Before practising the exercises, attend to your personal hygiene: empty your bladder and bowel; cleanse your mouth and nostrils (*see the Nasal Wash* in Chapter 9).

You may practise the breathing exercises about 15 minutes following the postures described in Chapter 6. After practising the breathing exercises, lie down and relax (as in the Pose of Tranquillity, *page 51*).

See Chapter 4 for directions on food and drink, and time and place to practise.

Avoid practising yoga postures immediately after a session of breathing exercises.

CAUTIONS

Do not practise the *dynamic version of the Cleansing Breath* if you have a heart condition, high blood pressure, epilepsy, an ear or eye problem or a hernia. *Do not* practise it during menstruation or if you are pregnant. (You may, however, try the simple Cleansing Breath instead.)

Do not hold your breath unless under the guidance of an experienced yoga teacher.

Also see Chapter 4 for general cautions.

THE EXERCISES

ALTERNATE NOSTRIL BREATHING

Benefits
This is a very soothing breathing exercise. It helps to alleviate anxiety (which aggravates both physical discomforts and pain) and is a useful antidote for sleeplessness.

How to Do It
1. Sit with your spine held naturally erect or properly supported. Relax your body, making

Alternate Nostril Breathing

a quick top-to-toe check. Relax your jaws. Breathe regularly through your nostrils.

2. Rest your left hand quietly in your lap, on your knee or on an armrest if you are sitting in an easy chair.

3. Arrange the fingers of your right hand as shown on page 73. Your right thumb is used to close your right nostril; your two middle fingers are curled towards the palm, and your little and ring fingers are used to close the left nostril. (Alternatively, you may rest your two middle fingers lightly above the bridge of your nose.)

4. Close your eyes and begin: close your right nostril and inhale slowly, smoothly and deeply through your left nostril.

5. Close your left nostril and release closure of your right; exhale.

6. Inhale through your right nostril.

7. Close your right nostril; release closure of your left and exhale. This completes one round of Alternate Nostril Breathing.

8. Repeat steps 4 to 7 in smooth succession, as many times as you wish, until you feel a sense of calm and wellbeing.

9. Relax your right arm and hand. Resume regular breathing. Open your eyes.

ANTI-ANXIETY BREATH

Benefits
This breathing exercise is superb for counteracting anxiety. It is one of my favourites, bringing me positive results in as little as two minutes. Practise it whenever you begin to feel harassed, frustrated, anxious or apprehensive. Use it as an antidote to a panic attack; you can also help someone else conquer such an attack by calmly instructing him or her to repeat steps 2 to 4 of this exercise, again and again, until the crisis has passed.

How to Do It
1. Sit comfortably. Close your eyes if it is safe to do so. Relax your jaws. (You may also practise this exercise while lying or standing.)

2. Inhale through your nostrils slowly, smoothly and as deeply as possible without strain. Breathe as quietly as you can.

3. Exhale steadily, focusing your attention on the area just above your navel.

4. *Before inhaling* again, mentally count 'one thousand', 'two thousand'. (The idea is to lengthen the exhalation phase of each respiration.)

5. Repeat steps 2 to 4, in smooth succession again and again, until you feel calm.

6. Resume normal breathing.

BREATHING AWAY PAIN

Benefits
By consciously slowing down your respirations, you become less tense. As tension diminishes, circulation improves so that a painful area of your body receives a better blood supply and pain-producing irritants are eliminated. Also, by focusing full attention on the breathing process, your awareness of pain is lessened.

Use this breathing technique to 'breathe away' fatigue and other unwelcome feelings.

How to Do It
1. Sit, or lie comfortably on your back, with your legs stretched out and comfortably separated. (With modification, you may also practise this exercise in The Crocodile position, *page 52*). Close your eyes, relax your jaws and breathe regularly.

2. Slow down your breathing, making it smoother and more even.

3. Rest your fingertips lightly on the area which is painful and take a long, steady inward breath. As you do so, visualize a

soothing jet of clear water flowing along your arm and hands towards your fingers. Imagine that the water contains healing properties that are being transmitted to the area in pain.

4. Breathe out steadily, visualizing irritants and impurities leaving the affected area on the outgoing breath.

5. Repeat steps 3 and 4, again and again, until you feel relief.

6. Relax your arms and hands, and rest.

Note. Use any appropriate imagery with which you feel comfortable. You may, for example, visualize a fine brush gently dusting away deposits from aching joints, each time you exhale. Or you can visualize your skin absorbing a healing balm, with each inhalation.

CLEANSING BREATH (DYNAMIC)

Cautions
Do not practise this exercise if you have a heart condition, high blood pressure, epilepsy, an ear or eye problem or a hernia. *Do not* practise it during menstruation or if you are pregnant. (You may, however, try the simple Cleansing Breath which follows.)

Benefits
Excellent for cleansing the respiratory passages, this exercise also strengthens your abdominal muscles and the muscles involved in breathing. It stimulates lung tissues, relaxes chest muscles, and gently and effectively massages abdominal organs. It also improves elimination and tones and revitalizes the nervous system.

How to Do It
1. Sit comfortably. Relax your arms and hands. Close your eyes if it is safe to do so. Relax your jaws. Breathe regularly. (You may also practise this exercise lying or standing.)

2. Inhale slowly, smoothly and as deeply as you can without strain.

3. Exhale briskly, as if sneezing, focusing attention on your abdomen which will tighten and flatten.

4. Inhalation will follow naturally, almost involuntarily.

5. Repeat steps 3 and 4, again and again, in rapid succession.

6. Resume normal breathing as you rest.

CLEANSING BREATH (SIMPLE)

Benefits
This exercise is splendid for managing stress and releasing pent-up emotion. Practise it whenever you feel tension building or when you sense frustration mounting and patience diminishing (for example, in difficult traffic conditions).

How to Do It
1. Sit comfortably. Relax your arms and hands. Close your eyes if it is safe to do so. Relax your jaws and breathe regularly.

2. Inhale through your nostrils, slowly, smoothly and as deeply as you can without strain.

3. Through pouted lips – as if whistling or cooling a hot drink – blow air out in a steady stream. Do this slowly, smoothly and with awareness.

4. When your exhalation is complete, repeat steps 2 and 3 again and again in smooth succession, until you feel calmer and more in control.

5. Resume normal breathing.

COMPLETE BREATH

Benefits
This exercise trains you to use your breathing apparatus to the fullest advantage (see general benefits outlined at the

beginning of the chapter). Like the other techniques in this chapter, it is also a superb stress-management tool.

How to Do It

1. Lie on your back, with your legs stretched out in front and comfortably separated. Bend your arms and rest the palms of your hands flat on your abdomen, so that the tips of your middle fingers meet above your navel. (You may also practise this exercise sitting or standing, or in The Crocodile position, page 52, duly modified.) Close your eyes and relax your jaws.
2. Begin with a slow, smooth inhalation through your nostrils, making it as deep as possible without strain. Focus your attention on the movements of your chest and abdomen: your ribcage will expand and your abdomen rise. Your fingers will separate.
3. Exhale slowly and steadily through your nostrils, again focusing attention on your chest and abdomen: your ribcage will relax and your abdomen flatten. Your middle fingers will again touch.
4. Repeat steps 2 and 3 in smooth succession for several minutes.
5. Relax your arms and hands. Breathe regularly.

COOLING BREATH

Benefits

The Cooling Breath is a useful exercise to practise when your body is overheated – during a fever, for example, or when the weather is very hot. It helps counteract certain cravings, such as for tobacco. It also promotes relaxation.

How to Do It

1. Sit comfortably. Relax your arms and hands. Close your eyes. Relax your jaws and breathe regularly. (You may also practise this

exercise lying or standing.)
2. Stick your tongue out, then curl it lengthways to form a sort of tube. Inhale slowly and steadily through this 'tube'.
3. Withdraw your tongue, relax your mouth and exhale steadily through your nostrils.
4. Repeat steps 2 and 3, in smooth succession, as many times as you wish.
5. Resume normal breathing as you rest.

HUMMING BREATH

Benefits

This is rather like meditation on sound. It calms the mind, soothes the spirit and relaxes the body.

How to Do It

1. Sit comfortably. Relax your arms and hands. Close your eyes. Relax your jaws and breathe regularly.
2. Inhale slowly, smoothly and as deeply as you can without strain.
3. As you exhale, slowly and steadily, make a humming sound which should last as long as your exhalation does. Pay full attention to this sound; become immersed in it.
4. Repeat steps 2 and 3, again and again in smooth succession, until you feel relaxed.
5. Resume normal breathing.

SIGHING BREATH

Benefits

The Sighing Breath is a very effective relaxant when your chest is tight and you cannot breathe deeply; it is a superb antidote for built-up tension. Practise this exercise when you are feeling anxious, upset or pressured.

How to Do It

1. Sit comfortably. Relax your arms and hands. Close your eyes. Relax your jaws.

(You may also practise this exercise lying or standing.)

2. Take two, three or more small, quick inward breaths (you are, in fact, breaking up one long inhalation). *Do not* strain.

3. Exhale steadily through your nostrils.

4. Repeat steps 2 and 3 again and again, until you are able to take one steady, deep inhalation with complete comfort.

5. Breathe regularly.

WHISPERING BREATH

Benefits

This is a marvellous exercise to practise if you suffer from asthma. It helps you to gain control of the muscles involved in breathing, especially your diaphragm, which plays an important part in breathing out. The exercise also helps improve concentration and promote relaxation.

How to Do It

You will need a lighted candle when you first start to practise this exercise.

1. Sit comfortably in front of a lighted candle. Relax your arms and hands. Relax your jaws. Breathe regularly.

2. Inhale through your nostrils slowly, smoothly and steadily.

3. Through pouted lips, very *slowly, gently and with control*, blow at the candle flame to make it flicker but *not* to put it out.

4. When your exhalation has ended, repeat steps 2 and 3 again and again, in smooth succession, until you begin to feel tired.

5. Rest. Breathe regularly.

Note. When you have mastered this technique, you can dispense with the candle, and simply imagine that you are blowing at the flame. You can then practise the exercise sitting, lying, standing or walking up a flight of stairs.

CHAPTER EIGHT

MEDITATIVE EXERCISES

The exercises outlined in Chapter 6 are meditative, in a sense, because they train you to direct and hold your attention on the doing of only one thing at a time. They are, however, a more active form of meditation than the techniques offered in this chapter, and are good preparation for them.

WHAT IS MEDITATION?

Meditation is, in simple terms, a technique used to quiet a restless mind and dissuade it from dwelling on a particular thought or idea. During meditation, you focus attention on only one object or activity to the exclusion of everything else. It is a natural device used to relax your conscious mind without dulling awareness – doctors call the meditative state 'restful alertness'.

More and more, doctors are recommending to their patients a period of daily meditation to help prevent or resolve a variety of health problems. These include heart disease, high blood pressure, migraine headaches, various nervous system disorders and stomach and intestinal ulcers. Be sure, however, to *check with your doctor*.

BENEFITS OF MEDITATING

Regular meditation practice helps dissolve and remove deep-rooted nervous tensions. Consequently, you become more at ease with yourself and others, as well as more confident and productive. Things which were formerly upsetting begin to lose their impact, appearing at least manageable and thus giving you some feeling of control.

Meditation is nature's tranquillizer. Meditate before an interview, a public appearance or before the children come home – any time you anticipate a demanding situation.

WHAT PRODUCES THE BENEFITS?

During meditation, both oxygen consumption and carbon dioxide elimination decrease markedly, without an alteration in their balance. This means that the circulatory system is functioning effectively. The heart's workload is decreased, and heart and breathing rates slow down, thus indicating a state of deep relaxation.

Skin resistance increases significantly during meditation, denoting a calm emotional state. The body's metabolic rate drops by about 20 per cent, with a corresponding fall in blood pressure, and lactate ion concentration in the blood (suspected of adversely affecting muscle tone and emotional states), decreases by about 33 per cent. Brain-wave recordings on an electro-encephalograph (EEG) also show an unusual abundance of alpha waves, which implies that the brain is alert yet wonderfully rested.

PREPARING TO MEDITATE

The ability to sit quietly for about 20 minutes at a time and to stay relaxed is an important prerequisite for successful meditation. I therefore suggest that you become conversant with the seated postures (such as the Perfect Posture, *page 37*, and the Pose of Tranquillity, *page 51*).

Always meditate before a meal so that the process of digestion does not interfere with concentration. Choose a quiet place where you are unlikely to be disturbed for about 20 minutes.

Sit comfortably, with your spine well aligned and supported if necessary. Rest your hands quietly in your lap, on your knees or on the armrest of a chair. Close your eyes. Relax your body from top to toe. Breathe regularly.

Plan on meditating at least once a day; twice preferably. Start with five or ten minutes, and gradually increase to 20 minutes per session.

Candle Concentration (*see Chapter 6, page 71*) is suggested as a good preparation for meditating.

A SIMPLE MEDITATION EXERCISE

1. Sit comfortably and relaxed, as just described. Close your eyes. Breathe regularly.
2. On an exhalation, mentally say 'one'.
3. Inhale.
4. Repeat steps 2 and 3 again and again. Whenever your attention strays, gently redirect it to your breathing and silent repetition of the word 'one'.
5. When you are ready to end your meditation, do so slowly: open your eyes and gently stretch or massage your limbs. Never rush.

Note. You may substitute any short word or phrase for 'one' (such as 'peace', 'relax', 'love and light', or a simple affirmation such as 'I feel calm' or 'I *will* be healed'.

When confronted with a challenging or perplexing situation, try to recall the peace you experienced during meditation. This will help you to maintain a certain detachment and give you a more realistic perspective. Remember also to check your breathing, slowing it down and making it smoother, if necessary.

MEDITATION ON SOUND

Practise the Humming Breath, described in Chapter 7, as a meditation on sound.

TOUCH MEDITATION

For this meditation you will need a small, pleasing object which you can hold in both hands (such as a figurine or fruit).

1. Sit as described in the section on preparing to meditate. Close your eyes and breathe regularly.
2. Use each exhalation to enhance your awareness of your sense of touch, and to keep you focused on the object in your hands. Should your thoughts stray, patiently guide them back to your meditation and breathing.
3. End your meditation slowly and with awareness.

A HEALING MEDITATION

Practise the Breathing Away Pain exercise (described in Chapter 7), using appropriate imagery and mental suggestion.

CHAPTER NINE ⟶

HYGIENIC PRACTICES

The techniques described in this, the final chapter of Part 2, complement the postures and breathing, relaxation and meditative exercises outlined in the previous chapters. Traditionally yogic discipline included cleansing practices known as *kriyas*. Among these were techniques to cleanse and strengthen the eyes and to improve concentration. I have, therefore, included eye exercises in this section to complement the *Eye Splashing* described. You will also find the *Perineal Exercise* which contributes to good pelvic health.

EYE EXERCISES

Benefits
The following eye exercises strengthen your eye muscles and build up their stamina. They improve circulation to your eyes, tone your optic (eye) nerve, and combat eyestrain. They also help to improve eyesight in some cases.

How to Do Them
1. Sit comfortably. Relax your shoulders, arms and hands. Relax your jaws. Breathe regularly throughout the exercises. (You may also, with modification where necessary, practise these exercises standing or lying.) Keep your head still as you do the eye movements.
2. Look up, then look straight ahead.

3. Look down, then look straight ahead.
4. Look to your right, then straight ahead.
5. Look to your left, then straight ahead.
6. Look diagonally up on your right side, then diagonally down on your left side.
7. Look up on your left side, then diagonally down on your right side. Look ahead. Remember to keep breathing regularly.
8. Move your eyes in a half-circle, looking upwards. Rest.
9. Move your eyes in a half-circle, looking downwards.
10. Slowly circle your eyes clockwise a few times. Rest
11. Slowly circle your eyes anticlockwise a few times. Rest.
12. Finish by palming your eyes for a few minutes (*see Chapter 6, page 71*).

FOCUSING EXERCISES
1. Look at a distant point, perhaps a tree top or church spire.
2. Slowly shift your gaze to a nearby object.
3. Repeat the eye movements several times, remembering to breathe regularly. Rest.

EYE SPLASHING

Benefits
Eye Splashing helps reduce tension built up in your eyes; it relaxes your eyes and relieves eyestrain.

How to Do It
- Bend over a basin of clean, cool water and gently splash the water into your open eyes a few times.
- Gently pat your closed eyes with a soft, clean towel to dry them.
- Rest for a few minutes, breathing regularly.

NASAL WASH

Benefits
The Nasal Wash is a safe, effective way to help keep your nasal passages clear and soothe the mucous membrane that lines them. It increases the tolerance of the nasal lining to various irritants, and is a splendid treatment for sinus problems and allergic rhinitis (as occurs in conditions such as hay fever).

Practise doing a nasal wash up to three times a day. Do it before you begin your daily yoga session.

How to Do It
- Dissolve a quarter of a teaspoon of salt in one cup of warm water. (This is approximately the concentration of sodium in blood and tissue fluids.)
- Put a little of the salt-water solution into a clean, cupped hand and *carefully* inhale some of it into one nostril, while closing the other with a thumb or index finger.
- Briskly, but *not* forcefully, breathe out to expel the liquid. Repeat the procedure.
- Repeat the whole process with the other nostril.

PERINEAL EXERCISE
The word 'perineal' refers to the perineum, which is the lowest part of the torso, between the anus and the external genitals.

Benefits
This exercise contributes to good pelvic health. It strengthens and firms the perineum (which helps support pelvic organs), and adds to the intensity and pleasure of sexual intercourse. It also combats stress-related incontinence of urine, in which urine dribbles involuntarily when you laugh heartily, cough, sneeze or run.

How to Do It
1. Sit, lie or stand comfortably. Breathe regularly.
2. Exhale and tighten your perineum (as if trying to prevent the passage of urine or a bowel movement).
3. Hold the tightening as long as your exhalation lasts.
4. Inhale and relax.
5. Repeat steps 2 to 4 once. Rest. You may repeat the exercise once now.
6. Repeat the exercise several times throughout the day.

Note. Practise the Perineal Exercise whenever you can do so conveniently: when travelling by bus, train or aeroplane; while waiting at traffic lights; in a queue; at boring parties and meetings – any place where you feel comfortable doing it. No one will know you are exercising.

SITZ BATH

Benefits
Excellent for alleviating pain and various discomforts in the pelvis, the sitz bath is also a good, natural treatment for the symptomatic relief of haemorrhoids. It is soothing and relaxing.

For maximum benefit, remain in the sitz bath for 10 to 20 minutes. You may repeat the bath several times a day.

How to prepare and Use It
- Fill a large, deep basin with enough water

so that when you sit in it your pelvis is submerged.

- The water temperature should be between 38°C and 46°C (100°F and 115°F). You can maintain this temperature by adding more warm water as needed.
- Ideally, your feet and legs should not be in the water; that is why a basin is more desirable than a bathtub.
- Keep your upper body warm to prevent chilling and consequent tightening of blood vessels.

TONGUE CLEANSING

Benefits
Regular practice of cleansing your tongue will help keep your breath fresh and your teeth and gums healthy. It may also prevent a sore throat from developing or worsening.

How to Do It
- You will need a metal teaspoon reserved only for this purpose. (A toothbrush is *not* recommended. Special metal tongue-scrapers are available in some places.)
- Exhale and stick your tongue out. With the teaspoon inverted, *gently* scrape away, from back to front, the accumulated deposits. Rinse the spoon under cool running water.
- Repeat the scraping once or twice, each time on an exhalation.
- Finish by thoroughly rinsing your mouth and flossing and brushing your teeth.
- Thoroughly clean the teaspoon, dry it and put it away for future use.

PART THREE

A–Z OF SYMPTOMS
AND TREATMENTS

SYMPTOMS AND
TREATMENTS

Symptoms are perceptible changes in the body or its functions which may indicate disease or a phase of disease. This section deals with the symptoms of a variety of health disorders, with references to exercises (postures) and healing nutrients.

The exercises help to prevent the disorders from arising or recurring, and are also of value in assisting a return to, and maintenance of, normal function. Described in detail in Chapter 6, each exercise is followed by a page number (or numbers) which refers to the appropriate illustration. Please remember to do warm-ups before, and cool-down exercises after the postures (*see Chapter 5*), and to review Chapter 4 on how to prepare for the exercises. All the breathing exercises are dealt with in Chapter 7, and the meditative exercises outlined in Chapter 8. The Perineal Exercise, Nasal Wash, Tongue Cleansing, Sitz Bath and Eye Exercises and Splashing are all described in Chapter 9.

You will find notes on the specific beneficial nutrients after most entries – their food sources are listed in Chapter 3. Please consult a nutritionist or other qualified health-care professional if you decide to use nutritional supplements. Remember also that *all* nutrients taken in through a wholesome diet work together to build health, and that *no one* particular nutrient is a panacea.

The treatments described in this section will help to mobilize your own natural resources – your inner healer – for maintaining good health or for regaining it. They are not intended as a substitute for competent medical care. It is imperative, in the case of all serious health problems (whether acute or longstanding) to *see a doctor* trained in orthodox medicine. I encourage you to combine the best that orthodox medicine has to offer with yoga therapy or other appropriate complementary therapy.

ACNE

(see also Skin Problems)

Acne is an inflammatory disease of the oil-secreting (sebaceous) glands and hair follicles of the skin, characterized by blackheads (comedones) and red elevated areas, some of which may contain pustules. Also called *acne vulgaris*, or common acne. Occurs mostly in adolescence.

Predisposing causes include heredity and hormonal disturbances. Food allergies, endocrine gland disorders, vitamin and mineral deficiencies and emotional disturbances are all aggravating factors.

Common sites are the face, neck, upper chest, back and shoulders.

Exercises

Pose of Tranquillity (*page 51*), Pose of a Child (*page 55*), Half Moon (*page 60*), Spinal Twist (*page 61*), Half Shoulderstand (*page 62*), Full Shoulderstand (*page 63*), Mock Headstand (*page 64*), Dog Stretch (*page 64*), Sun Salutations (*pages 65–68*), Alternate Nostril Breathing (*page 73*), Anti-Anxiety Breath (*page 74*), Cleansing Breath (Dynamic) (*page 75*), Complete Breath (*page 75*), Meditation.

Nutrients

Vitamin A, the B vitamins (particularly B_2, B_3, B_6, biotin, inositol, PABA), vitamins C, D, and E, EFAs, chromium, copper, magnesium, selenium, silicon, sulphur, zinc.

ADDICTION

A physical and/or psychological dependence on a substance – especially alcohol, drugs and tobacco – with use of increasing amounts.

Apart from providing pleasure, many substances create dependence by altering body chemistry. Cravings increase with habitual use of the substance and withdrawal symptoms occur when attempts are made to stop.

Yoga provides safer, alternative ways of dealing with stressors. It promotes a sense of self-control and assists in resisting the appeal of addictive substances. Yoga practices also help build self-confidence and the ability to deal with the guilt often inherent in recovering from addiction.

Exercises

Balance Posture (*page 45*), Chest Expander (*page 47*), Fish Posture (*page 49*), Pose of Tranquillity (*page 51*), Sun Salutations (*pages 65–68*), Alternate Nostril Breathing (*page 73*), Anti-Anxiety Breath (*page 74*), Cleansing Breath (Dynamic) (*page 75*), Complete Breath (*page 75*), Cooling Breath (*page 76*). Meditation.

Nutrients

Vitamin A, the B vitamins (particularly B_1, B_3, B_5, B_6, B_{15}), vitamins C and E, EFAs (omega-6 fatty acids), calcium, magnesium, selenium, zinc, carnitine.

AIDS (ACQUIRED IMMUNE DEFICIENCY SYNDROME)

(*see also Immune System Disorders*)

Generally attributed to infection by HIV (human immuno-deficiency virus), AIDS is usually a fatal disease.

Most cases of AIDS have developed after sexual contact with an HIV-infected person. Those most at risk are homosexuals and bisexuals, particularly those with multiple partners; heterosexual partners of persons with AIDS; intravenous drug users; haemophiliacs and others receiving multiple transfusions of blood or blood products; and male and female prostitutes. There are no reports of the AIDS virus having been spread via food, coughing or talking. Some evidence does exist, however, of it spreading via tears and saliva, and an infected woman could transmit the virus to her baby during pregnancy, at birth or through breastfeeding. There is, at present, no known cure for AIDS.

Yoga can help equip you to face more courageously the many emotional and physical challenges and trials that the disease may bring. In the Healing Meditation, for instance, you can visualize the cells of your immune system being strengthened, all the better to attack the diseased cells in your body. This will reinforce the feeling that you *are* doing something to help yourself and that you are not totally helpless.

If you are receiving chemotherapy, practising deep relaxation (Pose of Tranquillity) and repeating affirmations during meditation can be useful in helping to alleviate nausea and other unpleasant symptoms. You can visualize your own healthy cells assisting the chemicals to do their work more effectively.

By enabling the cells of the immune system to fight the disease more vigorously, yoga may possibly help delay the onset of full-blown AIDS. Once this occurs, however, and life expectancy is reduced, it can improve the quality of life and help to diminish suffering.

Exercises

If your energy and general condition permit, practise a few sets of Sun Salutations (*pages 65–68*), to begin with, followed by the Half Moon (*page 60*), Spinal Twist (*page 61*), Half Shoulderstand (*page 62*), or Full Shoulderstand (*page 63*). Finish the session(s) with the Pose of Tranquillity (*page 51*), or The Crocodile (*page 52*). All the breathing and meditative exercises are suitable for practice.

Nutrients

Vitamin A, carotenes, vitamin B complex, anti-stress factors, vitamin C and flavonoids, vitamin E, EFAs, calcium, copper, magnesium, selenium, zinc.

AIRSICKNESS

(*see Motion Sickness*)

ALCOHOLISM

(*see Addiction*)

ALLERGIC RHINITIS

(*see Allergies*)

ALLERGIES

(*see also Immune System Disorders and Nasal Allergy*)

An allergy is an acquired hypersensitivity to a substance (allergen) which does not normally cause a reaction. This reaction results from the release of histamine or histamine-like substances from injured cells. Allergy manifestations most commonly involve the respiratory tract or the skin.

Allergies may be inherited, or they may be triggered by pollen, dust, hair, fur, feathers, scales, wool, chemicals, drugs and insect bites; as well as by specific foods, such as eggs, chocolate, milk, wheat, tomatoes, citrus fruits, oatmeal and potatoes. Allergic symptoms are also often the body's response to stressors such as inadequate nutrition, insufficient sleep and infections.

Allergic conditions include: eczema, allergic rhinitis or coryza (headcold), hay fever, bronchial asthma, migraine, urticaria (hives), food allergies, intolerances and even mental disturbances.

Exercises

Mountain Posture (*page 40*), Cow Head Posture (*page 41*), Balance Posture (*page 45*), Chest Expander (*page 47*), Fish Posture (*page 49*), Pose of Tranquillity (*page 51*), The Crocodile (*page 52*), Spinal Twist (*page 61*),

Half Shoulderstand (*page 62*), Full Shoulderstand (*page 63*), Dog Stretch (*page 64*), Sun Salutations (*pages 65–68*), Alternate Nasal Breathing (*page 73*), Anti-Anxiety Breath, Cleansing Breath (Dynamic), Complete Breath. Nasal Wash.

Nutrients

Vitamin A, carotenes, the B vitamins (particularly B_3, B_5, B_6, B_{12}, B_{15}), vitamin C and flavonoids, vitamin E, EFAs, calcium copper, magnesium, selenium, zinc.

ALOPECIA (BALDNESS, HAIR LOSS)

Alopecia is the medical word for absence or loss of hair, especially on the head. The condition may occur as a result of a variety of causes, including: heredity; the ageing process; illnesses and infectious diseases; hormonal imbalance; nervous disorders or nervous system injury; toxic substances (such as drugs); excessive dandruff (seborrhoea); scalp injury or infection; impaired blood circulation; inadequate nutrition and stress.

Exercises

Abdominal Lift (*page 47*), Rock-and-Roll (*page 36*), Pose of Tranquillity (*page 51*), Pose of a Child (*page 55*), The Camel (*page 56*), The Bow (*page 59*), Half Shoulderstand (*page 62*), Full Shoulderstand (*page 63*), Mock Headstand (*page 64*), Dog Stretch (*page 64*), Alternate Nostril Breathing (*page 73*), Anti-Anxiety Breath, Cleansing Breath (Dynamic), Complete Breath. Meditation.

Nutrients

Vitamin A, the B vitamins (particularly B_5, B_9, biotin, inositol, PABA) anti-stress factors, EFAs, calcium, cobalt, copper, magnesium, selenium, zinc.

AMENORRHOEA

(*see Menstrual Irregularities*)

ANAEMIA

A condition in which there is a reduction in the number of circulating red blood cells, the amount of haemoglobin (the iron-containing pigment of red blood cells) or the volume of packed red cells per 100 millilitres of blood.

Anaemia is not itself a disease but rather a symptom of various disorders. It may be the result of excessive blood loss; excessive blood cell destruction or decreased blood cell formation – as occurs when the diet is iron deficient. Anaemia can also be caused by a dietary deficiency of copper, folic acid, vitamin C or vitamin B_{12}.

Symptoms of anaemia include: pallor of the skin, fingernail beds and mucous membranes; fatigue, weakness, dizziness, headache, rapid heartbeat, heart palpitation, chest pain, impaired sex drive and slight fever.

Exercises

Fish Posture (*page 49*), Pose of Tranquillity (*page 51*), Back-stretching Posture (*page 53*), The Cobra (*page 57*), Half Locust (*page 58*), Half Shoulderstand (*page 62*), Full Shoulderstand (*page 62*), Sun Salutations (*pages 65–68*), Complete Breath, Cooling Breath.

Nutrients

The B vitamins (particularly B_1, B_3, B_6, B_9, B_{12}, PABA) vitamins C, D, E, cobalt, copper, iron, magnesium, manganese, molybdenum, selenium, zinc.

ANGINA PECTORIS

(*see also Heart Disease and Pain*)

Angina pectoris is caused by an insufficient blood supply to the heart, and leads to severe pain and constriction near the heart. The pain usually radiates to the left shoulder and down the left arm, but may sometimes radiate to the back or the jaw.

Symptoms include: steady, severe pain and a feeling of pressure in the region of the heart; great anxiety; shortness of breath; fast and sometimes irregular pulse rate; elevated blood pressure. Exertion following a meal can produce angina symptoms and cold weather may also aggravate the condition.

Usually angina pain only lasts for a few minutes and generally occurs following (rather than at the same time as) physical exertion.

Associated symptoms may be related to low blood sugar (hypoglycaemia), emotional upset or a heart rhythm disorder (such as fibrillation).

Exercises

Pose of Tranquillity (*page 51*), Alternate Nostril Breathing (*page 73*), Anti-Anxiety Breath (*page 74*), Cleansing Breath (Simple), Complete Breath, Sighing Breath. Meditation.

Nutrients

Vitamin A, the B vitamins (particularly B_1, B_3, B_5, B_6, B_{15}, choline, inositol), vitamins C, D, E, EFAs, calcium, chromium, copper, magnesium, potassium, selenium, zinc, carnitine, lecithin.

ANKYLOSING SPONDYLITIS

(*see Arthritis*)

ANOREXIA

Anorexia (lack or loss of appetite) is seen in depression, malaise, fevers and various other illnesses; in stomach and intestinal disorders; and as a result of alcohol excess and drug addiction. It is also an undesired side effect of many medicines and medical procedures.

Anorexia nervosa occurs mostly in females between the ages of 12 and 21. It develops from an intense fear of being obese, and the fear does not diminish as weight loss progresses. Usually, there is no known physical illness to account for the weight loss.

Exercises

Pose of Tranquillity (*page 51*), Back-stretching Posture (*page 53*), The Cobra (*page 57*), Spinal Twist (*page 61*), Half Shoulderstand (*page 62*), Full Shoulderstand (*page 63*), Alternate Nostril Breathing (*page 73*), Anti-Anxiety Breath, Cleansing Breath (Simple), Complete Breath. Meditation.

Nutrients

Vitamin A, the B vitamins (particularly B_1, B_5, B_6, biotin, inositol), anti-stress factors, vitamins C, D, E, EFAs, calcium, iodine, magnesium, phosphorus, potassium, vanadium, zinc.

ANXIETY

Anxiety – a feeling of apprehension, worry, uneasiness or dread – is a normal reaction to a perceived threat to one's body, lifestyle, values or loved ones. Often it is not focused on a single identifiable cause.

Some anxiety is normal; it stimulates an individual to purposeful action. Excessive anxiety, however, interferes with the efficient functioning of a person.

Anxiety neurosis may be seen in some people without organic disease. Reported systems include: difficult breathing, heart pain and palpitations; various forms of muscle tension, including constriction of the throat and a band-like pressure about the head; feeling cold; hand tremors; sweating and agitation; nausea and diarrhoea; weakness and feeling faint; inability to think clearly.

Rapid breathing may lead to *hyperventilation* which in turn leads to *alkalosis*, in which body fluids become excessively alkaline.

Exercises

Pose of Tranquillity (*page 51*), Back-stretching Posture (*page 53*), The Plough (*page 54*), The Cobra (*page 57*), Spinal Twist (*page 61*), Sun Salutations (*pages 65–68*), Alternate Nostril Breathing (*page 73*), Anti-Anxiety Breath, Cleansing Breath (Dynamic), Cooling Breath, Humming Breath.

Nutrients

The B vitamins (particularly B_1, B_3, B_6, biotin, PABA), anti-stress factors, EFAs (omega-3 fatty acids), calcium, magnesium.

APPETITE LOSS

(*see Anorexia*)

ARTHRITIS

(*see also Autoimmune Disorders and Joint Disorders*)

Arthritis is the inflammation of a joint, and is usually accompanied by pain, swelling, and frequently a change in the joint's structure.

Arthritis may result from or be associated with a number of conditions, including: infection; rheumatic fever; ulcerative colitis; nervous system disorders; degenerative joint disease (such as osteoarthritis); metabolic disturbances (such as gout); new growths (neoplasms); inflammation of structures near the joints (such as bursitis); and a variety of other conditions (such as psoriasis and Raynaud's disease).

Ankylosing (rheumatoid) spondylitis is a chronic progressive disease of the joints, including the sacroiliac joints and those between the ribs and spine. Ankylosis (immobility and fixation of a joint) may give rise to a stiff back (poker spine).

Gout is a hereditary metabolic disease that is a form of acute arthritis. It is marked by inflammation of joints and usually begins in the knee or foot, but may also affect other joints.

Osteoarthritis (OA) is a chronic disease involving the joints, especially those bearing weight.

Rheumatism is a general term for acute and chronic conditions characterized by inflammation, soreness and stiffness of the muscles, and pain in joints and associated structures.

Rheumatoid arthritis (RA) is characterized by inflammatory changes in joints and related structures. It can result in crippling deformities, and is believed to be an immune system disorder which is poorly understood.

Exercises

Warm-ups (*pages 33–36*), Cow Head Posture (*page 41*), The Flower (*page 42*), Eagle Posture (*page 46*), Chest Expander (*page 47*), Pose of Tranquillity (*page 51*), Back-stretching Posture (*page 53*), The Plough (*page 54*), The Camel (*page 56*), The Cobra (*page 57*), The Bow (*page 59*), Lying Twist (*page 35*), Angle Posture (*page 61*), Spinal Twist (*page 61*), Sun Salutations (*pages 65–68*), Alternate Nostril Breathing (*page 73*), Anti-Anxiety Breath, Cleansing Breath (Dynamic), Cleansing Breath (Simple), Complete Breath. Meditation.

Nutrients

Vitamin A, carotenes, the B vitamins (particularly B_2, B_5), anti-stress factors, vitamin C, flavonoids, vitamins D, E, EFAs, boron, calcium, copper, iron, magnesium, manganese, selenium, silicon, zinc.
Note. Avoid foods and drinks known to interfere with the absorption of minerals, such as bran, coffee and tea.

ASTHMA

(*see also Allergies and Breathing Problems*)

Asthma involves sudden attacks of breathlessness accompanied by wheezing. It is caused by a spasm of the bronchial tubes or by swelling of their mucous membranes, with inflammation and the production of thick mucus. Attacks are sometimes triggered by emotional factors or mental and physical fatigue or stress.

Bronchial asthma, or *allergic asthma*, is a common form of asthma resulting from hypersensitivity to an allergen (any substance that produces symptoms of allergy).

Regular practice of yoga breathing techniques helps to develop the stamina of your respiratory system and, as you learn to use your breathing apparatus more effectively, your tense chest muscles (and other muscles used in breathing) relax. Energy blocks are released, giving you more energy, and breathing, relaxation and meditation techniques promote calm. Some yoga postures (chiefly the inverted postures) also facilitate the drainage of accumulating mucus.

In addition to helping to reduce the frequency of asthmatic attacks, regular yoga practice can be beneficial during an attack as it equips you to combat the vicious cycle of panic and respiratory distress that builds up. The increased ability to relax and control your breathing is also invaluable in preventing pains and in reducing the severity of the attack itself.

Exercises

Mountain Posture (*page 40*), Cow Head Posture (*page 41*), Chest Expander (*page 47*), Fish Posture (*page 49*), Pose of Tranquillity (*page 51*), The Crocodile (*page 52*), The Camel (*page 56*), The Cobra (*page 57*), The Bow (*page 59*), Angle Posture (*page 61*), Half Shoulderstand (*page 62*), Full Shoulderstand (*page 63*), slow performance of the Sun Salutations (*pages 65–68*), Alternate Nostril Breathing (*page 73*), Anti-Anxiety breath, Cleansing Breath (Dynamic), Complete Breath, Whispering Breath. Nasal Wash.

Nutrients

Vitamin A, the B vitamins (particularly B_6, B_9, B_{12}, B_{15}), anti-stress factors, vitamin C, flavonoids, vitamin E, EFAs, calcium, magnesium, selenium, zinc.
Note. Avoid monosodium glutamate (MSG) and additives with sulphur (such as metabisulphate and sulphur dioxide).

AUTOIMMUNE DISORDERS

(*see also Immune System Disorders*)

These are conditions in which the body produces disordered immunological responses against itself. Normally, the body's immune mechanisms are able to distinguish clearly between what is a normal substance and what is foreign. In autoimmune diseases, however, this system becomes defective and produces antibodies against normal parts of the body to such an extent as to cause tissue injury.

Factors contributing to the onset of autoimmune disease include: nutritional state, age, sex, race, heredity, radiation, alcohol intake, fatigue and stress. Autoimmune disease can also occur in response to infection and as a result of treatment with certain drugs.

Included in this category of disorders are rheumatoid arthritis, myasthenia gravis, scleroderma, arthritis, multiple sclerosis (MS) and lupus (systemic lupus erythematosus, or SLE).

Yoga can help you make the best of whatever muscular capacity you have. Often, this is greater than realized because when one group of muscles is impaired another group can take over. Yoga can also build needed courage to enable you to persevere with retraining exercises.

I personally witnessed the truth of these statements when I instructed yoga classes specially designed for people with MS. Some students amazed themselves at what they achieved by the end of the series of classes.

Through regular practice of meditation and breathing and relaxation exercises, beneficial nervous system changes can take place to delay further degeneration. Even when MS is advanced, yoga practices can help you gain a more realistic perspective and equip you to make the very best of existing circumstances.

Exercises

Start with gentle warm-ups and one or two sets of Sun Salutation (*pages 65–68*), performed slowly. Add The Tree (*page 44*), The Plough (*page 54*), Angle Posture (*page 61*), Spinal Twist (*page 61*), Half Shoulderstand (*page 62*), or Full Shoulderstand (*page 63*), if your condition permits it.

Daily practice of the Pose of Tranquillity (*page 51*) is recommended, as well as some form of meditation. Breathing exercises should include Alternate Nostril breathing (*page 73*), the Anti-Anxiety Breath, Cleansing Breath (Simple), Complete Breath, and the Sighing breath when you find deep breathing difficult. Nasal Wash.

Nutrients

Vitamin A, carotenes, the B vitamins (particularly B_1, B_2, B_3, B_5, B_6, B_9, B_{12}, B_{15}, choline, inositol), anti-stress factors, vitamin C, flavonoids, vitamin E, EFAs, calcium, copper, magnesium, manganese, molybdenum, vanadium, zinc, carnitine.

BACKACHE

Backache refers to pain in any of the areas on either side of the spinal column, from the base of the neck to the pelvis. Backache is usually characterized by dull, continuous pain and tenderness in the muscles and their attachments. Pain sometimes radiates to the legs, following the distribution of the sciatic nerve.

Causes of backache include: infection; tumours or other abnormality in any part of the body (the uterus or prostate gland, for example); disorders of the vertebral (spinal) column, such as abnormality of the discs between the vertebrae; bone fractures, such as those occurring as a result of degenerative bone diseases like osteoporosis; strains or sprains; inadequacy of the ligaments supporting the spine; muscle injury or spasm; inflammation of related structures; poor postural habits; and psychogenic (of mental origin) factors.

Lumbago is a general, non-specific word used to describe a dull ache in the lumbar (loin) part of the back.

Scolioisis is a lateral curvature of the spine, usually consisting of two curves: the original abnormal curve and a compensatory curve in the opposite direction.

Congenital scoliosis is present from birth and is usually the result of defective spinal development prior to birth.

Habit scoliosis results from habitually assuming improper body positions.

Myopathic scoliosis is due to a weakening of spinal muscles.

Rheumatic scoliosis is a result of rheumatism of the back muscles.

For detailed information on back care, including, for example, how to sit, stand, and lift correctly, please refer to my book entitled *The Yoga Back Book* (*see the Bibliography for details*).

Exercises

As a preventive measure, regularly practise the following when not in pain: Squatting Posture (*page 39*), Cow Head Posture (*page 41*), Angle Balance (*page 42*), Balance Posture (*page 45*), Chest Expander (*page 47*), Abdominal Lift (*page 47*), Supine Knee Squeeze (*page 49*), Legs Up (*page 50*), Pose of Tranquillity (*page 51*), Star Posture (*page 53*), Spread Leg Stretch (*page 54*), Pose of a Child (*page 55*), Triangle Posture (*page 55*), Pelvic Stretch (*page 56*), The Cobra (*page 57*), Half Locust (*page 58*), Angle Posture (*page 61*), Dog Stretch (*page 64*), Cat Stretch series (*pages 69–70*). Alternate Nostril Breathing (*page 73*), Anti-Anxiety Breath, Breathing Away Pain (practise when in pain), Cleansing Breath (Simple), Complete Breath, Sighing Breath.

Nutrients

Vitamin A, the B vitamins, anti-stress factors, vitamins C, D, E, calcium, fluorine, magnesium, phosphorus, silicon.

BALDNESS

(*see Alopecia*)

BLADDER PROBLEMS

(*see Cystitis, Incontinence of Urine and Urinary Problems*)

BLOOD PRESSURE (HIGH)

Blood pressure refers to the force exerted by the blood against the inner walls of the arteries as a result of the heart's pumping action.

Hypertension is a condition in which the blood pressure is higher than that judged to be normal.

Essential (primary) hypertension is that in which the precise cause is unknown.

Secondary hypertension results from an underlying disorder such as an adrenal gland tumour or kidney disease.

Because hypertension generally produces no symptoms, millions of people are unaware that they have the condition; it is usually discovered during a routine medical examination.

Untreated hypertension can lead to serious illness such as coronary artery disease, congestive heart failure, a stroke, aortic aneurysm or other cardiovascular (heart and blood vessels) disease.

Hypertension is one of the most difficult disorders to control since virtually any stressor will cause changes in blood pressure. The systolic arterial blood pressure, for instance, rises during activity and excitement (systolic refers to the pressure produced in the arteries by the push of blood as the heart's left lower chamber contracts).

For many years now, yoga breathing, relaxation and meditation techniques have been used successfully to help lower high blood pressure and keep it within normal limits. These techniques have also enabled some people to reduce medication dosages, and others to stop taking medication altogether – *with their doctor's approval.*

There is now little question that a learned blood pressure control through the regular practice of breathing, relaxation and meditation techniques can be sustained for long periods.

The Pose of Tranquillity is outstanding among the various exercises for helping to bring about these beneficial results.

Exercises

Pose of Tranquillity (*page 51*), Candle Concentration (*page 71*), Palming (*page 71*), Alternate Nostril Breathing (*page 73*), Anti-Anxiety Breath, Cleansing Breath (Simple), Complete Breath, Humming Breath. All the meditative exercises.

Nutrients

The B vitamins (particularly B_2, B_3, B_6, B_{15}, choline, inositol), anti-stress factors, vitamins C, D, E, EFAs, calcium, chromium, magnesium, potassium, vanadium, zinc, lecithin.

BREATHING PROBLEMS

Breathing, or respiration, may be described as the act of inhaling and exhaling air.

Exhalation is usually passive and takes less time than inhalation. When you breathe with passive exhalation, however, you do not move as much air in and out of your lungs as you can and should. The more air you move, the healthier you will be, because the functioning of all body systems depends on the delivery of oxygen in inspired air and the removal of carbon dioxide in expired air. To bring more air into your lungs, concentrate on expelling more air by attending to exhalation (*see the Anti-Anxiety Breath, Chapter 7*).

Various difficulties can arise during the breathing process. Here are a few:

Asthmatic breathing is harsh, with a prolonged wheezing expiration (breathing out) heard all over the chest.

Bronchial breathing is also harsh, with a prolonged, high-pitched exhalation.

Laboured breathing (dyspnoea) or gasping for

oxygen is normal when caused by strenuous exercise, but it may indicate a respiratory disorder of the amount of oxygen circulating in the blood when excessive, prolonged or occurring at rest.

A breathing difficulty may be a symptom of a variety of disorders, including chronic bronchitis, emphysema, cancer or heart disease.

Some conditions, such as allergies, chronic fatigue and respiratory infections can be caused by poor breathing habits.

Yoga retrains you to breathe efficiently. It promotes mental calm, which is useful in combating such conditions as bronchial asthma and nasal allergy. Yoga, moreover, helps to strengthen the immune system so that chronic infections are less liable to arise, but if they do, they tend to clear up quickly.

If your lungs are permanently damaged (as in chronic bronchitis), yoga practices help you to improve the mechanical efficiency of your breathing and to make the most of your reduced lung capacity. They also assist you to give up smoking.

In nasal allergy – characterized by excessive sneezing and a blocked or 'runny' nose – yoga breathing and other exercises, as well as the Nasal Wash, all help increase the tolerance of the nasal lining to irritants.

In chronic lung diseases, such as emphysema, although yoga cannot repair damaged tissues, it can enhance the effectiveness of physiotherapy and surgical and drug treatments. Yoga breathing techniques train you to oxygenate all parts of your lungs. Some postures (such as the inverted postures) also promote the drainage of secretions and improve stamina and general health.

As the efficiency of your breathing apparatus and your immune system increases, any drugs you may be using tend to become more effective, so that smaller doses may be required. Always *check with your doctor* before reducing medication dosages.

Apart from physical improvement brought about by diligent practice of yoga *asanas* and breathing exercises, functional capacity is increased and the degree of tissue damage kept to a minimum.

Finally, as a means of mental mastery, yoga can help you to give up smoking, which is vital in the case of severe lung damage – as occurs in chronic bronchitis and emphysema, to name but two conditions.

Exercises

Mountain Posture (*page 40*), Cow Head Posture (*page 41*), Chest Expander (*page 47*), Fish Posture (*page 49*), Pose of Tranquillity (*page 51*), The Crocodile (*page 52*), The Camel (*page 56*), The Cobra (*page 57*), The Bow (*page 59*), Half Shoulderstand (*page 62*), Full Shoulderstand (*page 63*), Alternate Nostril Breathing (*page 73*). Anti-Anxiety Breath, Cleansing Breath (Simple), Complete Breath, Sighing Breath, Whispering Breath, Meditation. Nasal Wash.

Nutrients

Vitamin A, carotenes, the B vitamins (particularly B_6, B_9, B_{12}, B_{15}), anti-stress factors, vitamin C, flavonoids, vitamin E, EFAs, calcium, magnesium, phosphorus, selenium, zinc.

BRONCHIAL ASTHMA

(*see Asthma*)

BRONCHITIS

(*see Breathing Problems*)

BRUXISM

Bruxism – the grinding of teeth, especially during sleep – is more than just an unpleasant habit; it can lead to damage to teeth, gums, jaw joints (*see TMJ Syndrome*) and muscles.

Exercises

Tension-relieving neck and shoulder exercises (Chapter 5). Be aware of jaw tension building up; unclench your teeth. Practise The Lion (*page 43*), after doing neck and shoulder warm-ups. Practise the Pose of Tranquillity (*page 51*), daily, as well as breathing exercises: Anti-Anxiety Breath, Cleansing Breath (Simple), Complete Breath, Humming Breath, Sighing Breath. Meditation.

Nutrients

The B vitamins (particularly B_5), anti-stress factors, calcium, magnesium.

CANCER

(*see also AIDS*)

Cancer comprises a broad group of malignant tumours which are divided into two categories: carcinomas and sarcomas. Carcinomas originate in epithelial cells forming outer body surfaces (such as skin), and in cavities and principal tubes and passages leading to the exterior (such as the uterus). Sarcomas develop from connective tissue, such as bone and muscle.

Cancer is invasive and tends to metastasize (transfer from one part of the body to another, not directly connected). It spreads directly into surrounding tissues and may also be disseminated through the lymphatic and circulatory systems.

The exact cause of cancer in humans is unknown. Contributing factors, however, include chronic irritation, nutritional considerations, radiation, heredity and a variety of chemicals.

You can help prevent many cancers by changing your lifestyle and certain habits. For example, smoking, excessive alcohol consumption, chronic constipation and prolonged stress are all cancer inducing. With regular yoga practice you can gain control over the craving for pleasure through harmful activities that put you at risk of cancer.

If cancer does develop, yoga practices will be a useful adjunct to surgery, chemotherapy and radiotherapy. They can also be an aid to rehabilitation after surgery, bur first *check with your doctor*.

Many cancer treatment facilities are now recommending visualization as a complement to standard medical cancer treatments. Visualization is based on principles of psychoneuroimmunology (referring to the nervous, immune and endocrine systems): what the mind visualizes can be carried out by the immune system – the body's natural weapon against cancer.

Exercises

Practise, in slow motion, one or two sets of Sun Salutations (*pages 65–68*), daily or twice daily to begin with; increase the number of times according to your general condition and energy level. Follow these with the Half Moon (*page 60*), Spinal Twist (*page 61*), Half Shoulderstand (*page 62*), or Full Shoulderstand (*page 63*). Finish the session(s) with the Pose of Tranquillity (*page 51*), or The Crocodile (*page 52*). All the breathing and meditative exercises are suitable for practice. Include Candle

Concentration (*page 71*), and Alternate
Nostril Breathing (*page 73*).

Nutrients

Vitamin A, carotenes, the B vitamins
(particularly B_3, B_6, B_9), anti-stress factors,
vitamin C, flavonoids, vitamins D, E, EFAs,
calcium, copper, magnesium, selenium, zinc,
dietary fibre.

CATARRH

(*see also Breathing Problems*)

Catarrh is a basic inflammation of the
mucous membranes, usually resulting in an
increased secretion of mucus.

Dry catarrh refers to severe coughing spells,
often seen in the elderly, and generally in
association with emphysema or asthma.

Exercises

Mountain Posture (*page 40*), Cow Head
Posture (*page 41*), The Lion (*page 43*), Chest
Expander (*page 47*), Fish posture (*page 49*),
Pose of Tranquillity (*page 51*), The Crocodile
(*page 52*). Alternate Nostril Breathing (*page
73*). All the breathing exercises are suitable.
Nasal Wash.

Nutrients

Vitamin A, carotenes, the B vitamins, anti-
stress factors, vitamin C, flavonoids, vitamins
D, E, EFAs, calcium, magnesium, selenium,
zinc.

CHEST PAIN

(*see Angina Pectoris*)

CHRONIC FATIGUE SYNDROME

(*see ME*)

CHRONIC LUNG DISEASE

(*see Breathing Problems*)

COLDS

(*see also Allergies, Breathing Problems and Nasal
Allergy*)

A general term for coryza or inflammation of
the respiratory mucous membranes, known
as the common cold.

Chest cold refers to a cold with inflammation of the bronchial mucous membranes. It
is a synonym for bronchitis.

Common cold denotes an acute catarrhal
inflammation of any or all parts of the
respiratory tract. It is highly contagious, and
caused by any one of a considerable number
of viruses.

Exercises

Yoga practices can help reduce the frequency
and severity of colds by strengthening the
immune system. Suitable exercises include
the Mountain Posture (*page 40*), Cow Head
Posture (*page 41*), The Lion (*page 43*),
(particularly for a sore throat), Chest Expander
(*page 47*), Fish Posture (*page 49*), Pose of
Tranquillity (*page 51*), and The Crocodile (*page
52*). Alternate Nostril Breathing (*page 73*). All
the breathing exercises are also appropriate.
Nasal Wash, Tongue Cleansing.

Nutrients

Vitamin A, carotenes, the B vitamins, anti-
stress factors, vitamin C, flavonoids, vitamins

D, E, EFAs, calcium, copper, iron, magnesium, potassium, selenium, zinc.

CONSTIPATION

Constipation denotes difficult defaecation (evacuation of the bowels), or infrequent defaecation, with the passage of unusually hard or dry faecal material. It involves a sluggish action of the bowels.

It is impossible to state accurately how often the bowels should move and so to determine what is normal. The range in healthy people can vary from two to three bowels movements a day to two per week.

Factors contributing to constipation include: no regular bowel movements from childhood; failure to establish definite and regular times for bowel movements; worry, anxiety or fear; a sedentary lifestyle; inadequate fluid intake; inadequate diet; internal obstruction; tumours; excessive use of laxatives; weakness of intestinal muscles; use of certain drugs; and lesions (injury or infection) of the anus.

Note. A continuous change in the frequency of bowel movements may be a sign of serious intestinal or colonic disease. *A change in bowel habits should be discussed with a doctor.*

Exercises

Efficiency bowel function depends, to a great extent, on the tone of the abdominal muscles and those of the rectum and anus. Squatting Posture (*page 39*), Angle Balance (*page 42*), Abdominal Lift (*page 47*), Stick Posture (*page 48*), Supine Knee Squeeze (*page 49*), Fish Posture (*page 49*), Pose of Tranquillity (*page 51*), The Crocodile (*page 52*), Back-stretching Posture (*page 53*), The Plough (*page 54*), Pose of a Child (*page 55*), The Camel (*page 56*), The Cobra (*page 57*),

The Bow (*page 59*), Lying Twist (*page 35*), Half Moon (*page 60*), Angle Posture (*page 61*), Spinal Twist (*page 61*), Half Shoulderstand (*page 62*), Full Shoulderstand (*page 63*), Sun Salutations (*pages 65–68*), Perineal Exercise. Anti-Anxiety Breath, Cleansing Breath (Dynamic), Complete Breath.

Nutrients

The B vitamins (particularly B_1, B_5, B_9, choline, inositol, PABA), vitamin C, magnesium, potassium, dietary fibre. Drink plenty of water.

COUGH

(see also Breathing Problems)

A cough may result from a variety of conditions, such as asthma, bronchiectasis, bronchitis, tuberculosis and pneumonia.

It is usually inadvisable to suppress coughs completely as this may lead to inflammation of the respiratory tract, particularly if sputum is produced by the coughing.

Exercises

Mountain Posture (*page 40*), Cow Head Posture (*page 41*), Chest Expander (*page 47*), Fish Posture (*page 49*), Pose of Tranquillity (*page 51*), Half Shoulderstand (*page 62*), Full Shoulderstand (*page 63*), Alternate Nasal Breathing (*page 73*). Anti-Anxiety Breath, Cleansing Breath (Simple), Complete Breath, Sighing Breath. Nasal Wash.

Nutrients

Vitamin A, carotenes, the B vitamins, anti-stress factors, vitamin C, flavonoids, vitamins D and E, EFAs, calcium, magnesium, selenium, zinc.

CRAMP

(see also Menstrual Irregularities and Pain)

Cramp is a spasmodic contraction of one or many muscles, usually painful. It may be caused by heat, cold or fatigue. Some cramps may also be a symptom of disease, such as chronic kidney failure.

In certain occupations, the habitual exercise of certain muscle groups may lead to so-called 'professional cramp'.

Writer's cramp is when the attempt to write induces a painful spasm of the hand muscles.

Depending on the cause and location, trying to extend the muscle sometimes helps. The application of cold or heat is also useful.

Exercises

To improve circulation and prevent cramp, regularly practise the following for leg cramp: Ankle Rotation (Chapter 5), Rock-and Roll (*page 36*), Legs Up (*page 50*), Pose of Tranquillity (*page 51*), Back-Stretching Posture (*page 53*), Star Posture (*page 53*), Spread Leg Stretch (*page 54*), The Plough (*page 54*), Pose of a Child (*page 55*), Pelvic Stretch (*page 56*), Lying Twist (*page 35*), Side Leg Raise (*page 59*), Spinal Twist (*page 61*), Cat Stretch series (*pages 69–70*), and, when not menstruating, the Half Shoulderstand (*page 62*), or Full Shoulderstand (*page 63*). Alternate Nostril Breathing (*page 73*). Anti-Anxiety Breath, Breathing Away Pain (to relieve cramp) and the Complete Breath.

Nutrients

The B vitamins (particularly B_1, B_2, B_3, B_5, B_6, biotin) anti-stress factors, vitamins C, D, E, EFAs (omega-6 fatty acids), calcium, magnesium, potassium, sodium, zinc.

CROHN'S DISEASE

(see Inflammatory Bowel Disease)

(CTS) CARPAL-TUNNEL SYNDROME

(see also Pain)

CTS is caused by pressure on the median nerve at the point where it goes through the carpal (wrist bone) tunnel. It can lead to soreness, tenderness and weakness of the thumb muscles, and to numbness or tingling in the forearm, and weakness of the fingers or an inability to bend them.

The compression of the median nerve may be caused by any of a dozen factors, ranging from arthritis to being overweight. Any inflammation or abnormality that reduces space in the carpal tunnel and puts pressure on the nerve can give rise to CTS.

This condition is sometimes associated with symptoms in other parts of the body, such as fluctuating swelling of the feet or ankles, muscle spasms in the arms or legs at night, or pain in the elbows shoulders or knees.

Exercises

Practise daily rotation of your wrists, in both directions. Go through the shoulder warm-ups in Chapter 5. Follow these with The Flower (*page 42*), and finish by shaking imaginary drops of water from your hands, then fully stretching your arms sideways. Also practise daily in the pose of Tranquillity (*page 51*), to keep the build-up of tension to a minimum. All the breathing and meditative exercises are suitable for practice.

Nutrients

The B vitamins (particularly B_2, B_6, B_9), anti-stress factors, calcium, magnesium.

CYSTITIS

(*see also Incontinence of Urine and Urinary Problems*)

Cystitis is an inflammation of the bladder or the ureters, which carry urine from the kidneys to the bladder.

Symptoms of acute cystitis include: frequent and painful urination; a feeling of urgency to urinate; low back pain; pain above the pubic area; and blood in the urine.

Causes of cystitis cover bacterial infection, tumour or kidney stones.

Exercises

Butterfly (*page 34*), Squatting Posture (*page 39*), Knee and Thigh Stretch (*page 39*), Pose of Tranquillity (*page 51*), Star Posture (*page 53*), Spread Leg Stretch (*page 54*), The Plough (*page 54*), Pelvic Stretch (*page 56*), The Camel (*page 56*), The Cobra (*page 57*), Half Locust (*page 58*), The Bow (*page 59*), Side Leg Raise (*page 59*), Spinal Twist (*page 61*), Cat Stretch series (*pages 69–70*), Anti-Anxiety Breath, Breathing Away Pain (for pain relief), Cleansing Breath (Simple), Complete Breath.

Nutrients

Vitamin A, carotenes, the B vitamins (particularly B_2, B_5, B_6, B_9, B_{12}, choline, PABA), anti-stress factors, vitamin C, flavonoids, vitamins D, E, EFAs (omega-3 fatty acids), calcium, magnesium, selenium, zinc.

DANDRUFF

(*see Alopecia*)

DEPRESSION

(*see also Anxiety, Fatigue, Insomnia and Stress*)

Mental depression is characterized by extreme gloom. Diagnostic criteria include the presence of at least four of the following, every day for at least two weeks: poor appetite or significant weight loss or weight gain; insomnia or sleeping too much; increased or decreased activity; loss of interest or pleasure in usual activities or decreased sex drive; loss of energy and fatigue; feelings of worthlessness, self-reproach or inappropriate guilt; poor concentration; recurring thoughts of death, or suicidal thoughts.

Depression is a complex condition which may occur independent of, or together with, a physical illness: perhaps as a result of a viral or bacterial infection; a reaction to the use of any of dozens of drugs; or following the loss of someone or something that has been significant in one's life. It may also arise because of a genetic predisposition.

Exercises

Graduate exercises according to your energy level. Start with the warm-ups. Add one or two sets of Sun Salutations (*pages 65–68*), performed in slow motion. Practise daily the Pose of Tranquillity (*page 51*). When appropriate, add the Angle Balance (*page 42*), The Tree (*page 44*), Balance Posture (*page 45*), Chest Expander (*page 47*), The Plough (*page 54*), The Cobra (*page 57*), Spinal Twist (*page 61*), Half Shoulderstand (*page 62*), Full Shoulderstand (*page 63*). Also practise daily

Candle Concentration (*page 71*), Alternate Nostril Breathing (*page 73*), Anti-Anxiety Breath, Cleansing Breath (Dynamic), Complete Breath.

Nutrients

The B vitamins (particularly B_1, B_2, B_3, B_5, B_6, B_9, B_{12}, biotin, choline, inositol, PABA), anti-stress factors, vitamin C, calcium, iron, magnesium, potassium, zinc.

DERMATITIS

(*see Skin Problems*)

DIABETES MELLITUS

(*see also Heart Problems and Obesity*)
Diabetes is a disorder of carbohydrate metabolism, characterized by high blood sugar and glucose (sugar) in the urine.

Although the basic cause of diabetes is still unknown, the direct cause is the failure of beta cells of the pancreas to secrete an adequate amount of insulin. In most instances, diabetes mellitus is the result of a genetic disorder; but it may also result from a deficiency of beta cells, caused by inflammation, malignancy or surgery.

In addition to the danger of becoming acutely ill from abnormal blood sugar levels, diabetics are also at risk of potentially serious long-term complications affecting blood vessels, nerves and major body organs.

The incidence of diabetes mellitus rises sharply after middle age. However, much of the glucose intolerance among older adults is caused by a resistance of the body's tissues to the action of insulin, and not by a failure of the pancreas to secrete enough insulin. This condition is aggravated by obesity and can often be corrected by weight reduction and exercise.

Yoga can be very useful as a supplement to conventional therapy for diabetes. The self-discipline it teaches helps make diet control and weight reduction easier, and relaxation techniques reduce stress hormone levels and improve the function of the pancreas and the immune system.

Exercises

Cow Head Posture (*page 41*), Stick Posture (*page 48*), Fish Posture (*page 49*), Pose of Tranquillity (*page 51*), The Crocodile (*page 52*), Back-stretching Posture (*page 53*), The Plough (*page 54*), Pose of a Child (*page 55*), The Cobra (*page 57*), The Bow (*page 59*), Spinal Twist (*page 61*), Half Shoulderstand (*page 62*), Full Shoulderstand (*page 63*), Sun Salutations (*pages 65–68*). Alternate Nostril Breathing (*page 73*). Anti-Anxiety Breath, Cleansing Breath (Dynamic and Simple), Complete Breath, Humming Breath.

Nutrients

Vitamin A, carotenes, the B vitamins (particularly B_1, B_2, B_3, B_5, B_6, B_{12}, inositol), anti-stress factors, vitamin C, flavonoids, vitamin E, EFAs (omega-6 fatty acids), chromium, copper, iodine, manganese, phosphorus, potassium, selenium, zinc, carnitine, dietary fibre.

Note. Taking any supplement that can affect blood sugar regulation is *potentially dangerous*, especially in diabetics needing insulin. Such supplements should be taken only under the direction of someone knowledgeable in nutritional medicine.

DIARRHOEA

(*see also Inflammatory Bowel Disease and Irritable Bowel Syndrome*)

Diarrhoea is characterized by the frequent passage of unformed, watery bowel movements. It is a common symptom of gastrointestinal (stomach and intestines) disturbances.

Causes include faulty diet, inflammation or irritation of the lining of the intestines, gastrointestinal infections, certain drugs and emotional factors. Regular bouts of diarrhoea are also often related to anxiety and other forms of stress.

Exercises

Pose of Tranquillity (*page 51*), The Crocodile (*page 52*), Alternative Nostril Breathing (*page 73*), Anti-Anxiety Breath, Breathing Away Pain (for pain relief), Cleansing Breath (Simple), Sighing Breath.

Nutrients

The B vitamins (particularly B_1, B_3, B_6, B_9), anti-stress factors, magnesium, potassium, lecithin.

DIZZINESS

A sensation of loss of balance, with accompanying symptoms which include feeling faint, nausea, giddiness, blurred vision and weakness of the legs.

Causes of dizziness include: a sudden draining of blood from the head when arising from a lying or sitting position (orthostatic hypotension); a small stroke; central nervous system disease; heart disorders; abnormality of the inner ear, where the sense of balance is controlled; certain drugs; sunstroke and food poisoning.

Exercises

To develop good concentration and balance, regularly practise the Angle Balance (*page 42*), The Tree (*page 44*), Balance Posture (*page 45*), The Eagle (*page 46*) and Candle Concentration (*page 71*). Practise also the Pose of Tranquillity (*page 51*), Alternate Nostril Breathing (*page 73*), Anti-Anxiety Breath and the Complete Breath.

Nutrients

The B vitamins (particularly B_3, B_5, B_6, B_9, B_{12}, choline), vitamin C, flavonoids, iron, potassium.

DRUG DEPENDENCE

(*see Addiction*)

DRY-EYE SYNDROME (SJÖGREN'S DISEASE)

(*see also Arthritis and Autoimmune Disorders*)

A syndrome occurring in postmenopausal women, symptoms of which include rheumatoid arthritis, dry mouth and dry eyes.

Other symptoms which may occur as part of this syndrome are increased dental caries, dryness of the vagina, loss of scalp hair and disturbances of the heart, lungs, kidneys, nervous and digestive systems. The dominant feature of these disturbances is tissue dehydration, and so adequate fluid intake is essential.

Dry-eye syndrome is thought to be a form of collagen disease (collagen is a cement-like substance that holds tissue cells together).

Exercises

Neck warm-ups (*page 33*), Pose of Tranquillity (*page 51*), Spinal Twist (*page 61*), Half Shoulderstand (*page 62*), Full Shoulderstand (*page 63*), Sun Salutations (*pages 65–68*), Candle Concentration (*page 71*), Palming (*page 70*), Alternate Nostril Breathing (*page 73*), Cleansing Breath (Simple), Complete Breath. Eye exercises and Eye Splashing.

Nutrients

Vitamin A, carotenes, the B vitamins (particularly B_2, B_6), vitamin C, flavonoids, vitamin E, EFAs (omega-6 fatty acids), selenium, silicon, zinc.

DUODENAL ULCER

(*see Ulcers*)

DYSEMENORRHOEA

(*See Menstrual Irregularities*)

DYSPEPSIA

(*see Stomach Disorders*)

ECZEMA

(*see Skin Problems*)

EMOTIONAL STRESS

(*see Stress*)

EMPHYSEMA

(*see also Breathing Problems*)

Emphysema is a chronic lung disease characterized by overinflation of the air sacs (alveoli) and by destruction of their walls. This gradual deterioration of the alveoli reduces the elasticity of the lungs and the amount of the oxygen that can be absorbed with each breath. The lungs are in a constant state of inflation because of difficulty exhaling.

Common causes of emphysema are cigarette smoking and chronic exposure to air pollutants, particularly dust and fumes.

Symptoms of emphysema include a breathlessness from levels of physical exertion that would have no effect on healthy people. Any effort involving the lungs – even laughing and shouting – can precipitate a coughing spell which may produce thick phlegm.

Exercises

Mountain Posture (*page 40*), Cow Head Posture (*page 41*), Chest Expander (*page 47*), Fish Posture (*page 49*), Pose of Tranquillity (*page 51*), The Crocodile (*page 52*), The Camel (*page 56*), The Cobra (*page 57*), The Bow (*page 59*), Half Shoulderstand (*page 62*), Full Shoulderstand (*page 63*), Alternate Nostril Breathing (*page 73*). Anti-Anxiety Breath. Nasal Wash.

Nutrients

Vitamin A, carotenes, the B vitamins (particularly B_6, B_9, B_{12}, B_{15}), anti-stress factors, vitamin C, flavonoids, vitamin E, EFAs, calcium, magnesium, selenium, zinc.

ENDOMETRIOSIS

(*see also Menstrual Irregularities*)

Uterine lining (endometrium) abnormally present in areas other than in the uterus – such as in the pelvis or abdominal wall – is known as endometriosis. Although the condition is not unusual in young women, 75 per cent of women with endometriosis are between the ages of 25 and 45.

Symptoms include painful menstrual periods (dysmenorrhoea), pain during sexual intercourse, stomach and intestinal symptoms, urinary symptoms and infertility. Breast pain is another, not uncommon, symptom of endometriosis and has been linked to an imbalance of essential fatty acids (EFAs).

Exercises

The Butterfly (*page 34*), Squatting Posture (*page 39*), Knee and Thigh Stretch (*page 39*), Mountain Posture (*page 40*), Chest Expander (*page 47*), Stick Posture (*page 48*), Supine Knee Squeeze (*page 49*), Legs Up (*page 50*), Pose of Tranquillity (*page 51*), The Crocodile (*page 52*), Star Posture (*page 53*), Spread Leg Stretch (*page 54*), Pose of a Child (*page 55*), Pelvic Stretch (*page 56*), Lying Twist (*page 35*), Side Leg Raise (*page 59*), Half Moon (*page 60*), Spinal Twist (*page 61*), When *not* menstruating, the Half Shoulderstand (*page 62*), and/or Full Shoulderstand (*page 63*). Cat Stretch series (*pages 69–70*). Alternate Nostril Breathing (*page 73*). Breathing Away Pain (for pain relief), Complete Breath, Humming Breath. Meditation.

Nutrients

The B vitamins (particularly B_3, B_6), vitamins C, E, EFAs, calcium, chromium, iodine, iron, magnesium, manganese, zinc.

EPILEPSY

Epilepsy is a nervous system disorder characterized by recurrent episodes of convulsive seizures and loss of consciousness.

There are about 20 different types of epilepsy, but the seizures commonly follow a pattern of loss of consciousness followed by jerking movements of the arms and legs. They are believed to be triggered by abnormal electrical discharge from a small area of diseased or injured brain tissue.

Although the diagnosis of epilepsy is usually made in childhood, an increasing proportion of cases are now being diagnosed after the age of 50. Epilepsy that develops in older adults may be caused by tumour, stroke, head injury or brain infection.

The orthodox treatment for epilepsy involves anticonvulsant medication to control the seizures.

Since the frequency of seizures is increased by stress and overbreathing (hyperventilation), yoga can play a vital therapeutic role. In particular, regular practice of controlled breathing techniques will train you not to hyperventilate, not to panic, and to maintain some balance during stressful situations. As you become adept at these breathing exercises you may, *with your doctor's permission*, be able to take a reduced dose of anti-seizure medications, which have the potential to produce undesirable side effects.

Exercises

Neck warm-ups. Pose of Tranquillity (*page 51*), The Crocodile (*page 52*). Alternate Nostril Breathing (*page 73*). Anti-Anxiety Breath, Complete Breath, Whispering Breath. Meditation.

Nutrients

The B vitamins (particularly B_2, B_3, B_5, B_6, biotin), calcium, magnesium.

EYESTRAIN

A tiredness of the eyes through overuse. Stress, pollution and spending a great deal of time in front of computer monitors can all lead to eyestrain. Eyestrain, in turn, can result in other eye problems such as allergic eye inflammations, and headaches are another possible consequence.

Conscious care of your eyes can help reduce eyestrain to a minimum and so limit its potential for damage. If problems already exist, yoga therapeutic practices can bring improvement and help slow down the rate of deterioration of eyesight.

The key to improvement is relaxation. Eye muscles – like muscles elsewhere in the body – respond to stress by overcontracting. Overcontraction of eye muscles can impair focusing and distort the shape of the eyeball; it may also worsen other existing eye problems. General relaxation of the body, as well as yoga eye exercises, help to reduce tension and strain, and build up the stamina of eye muscles.

Asanas that exercise the neck or change the pressure of blood to the head help prevent the build-up of tension. Cleansing practices such as the Nasal Wash relieve pressure in the sinuses. Palming (*page 71*), promotes relaxation of the eyes themselves, and Candle Concentration (*page 71*), beneficially stimulates the eyes and calms the mind. Focusing exercises train the eyes and assist in making visual adjustments, which is useful for those who read a great deal or work at computer monitors. They also improve mental and visual awareness.

Finally, Eye Splashing helps reduce tension built up in the eyes and so relaxes them.

Exercises

Neck warm-ups. Pose of Tranquillity (*page 51*), The Crocodile (*page 52*), Pose of a Child (*page 55*), Candle Concentration (*page 71*), Palming (*page 71*), Alternate Nostril Breathing (*page 73*). Eye exercises, Eye Splashing, Nasal Wash.

Nutrients

Vitamin A, the B vitamins (particularly B_2, inositol), vitamins C, D, E, zinc.

FATIGUE

(*see also Depression, Insomnia and ME*)

Fatigue denotes a feeling of tiredness or weariness, loss of strength or exhaustion. It may occur as a result of a variety of causes including: excessive activity; malnutrition (deficiency of carbohydrates, proteins, minerals or vitamins); circulatory disturbances, such as heart disease or anaemia, which interfere with the supply of oxygen and energy materials to tissues; respiratory disturbances; infectious diseases; endocrine gland disturbances, such as occur in diabetes and menopause; psychogenic factors such as emotional conflicts and anxiety; physical impairment and environmental noise.

Chronic fatigue is long-continued fatigue which is not relieved by rest. It is usually indicative of diseases such as tuberculosis or diabetes, or other conditions of altered body metabolism.

Neurasthenia is a term previously used to describe unexplained chronic fatigue and lassitude, with additional symptoms such as nervousness, irritability, anxiety, depression, headache, insomnia and sexual disorders. It is thought to result from an emotional rather than a physical disorder.

Exercises

Plan your exercise programme to help build up energy gradually: start with warm-ups and short walks. As energy increases, add one or two sets of Sun Salutations (*pages 65–68*), performed slowly. Also suggested is the daily practice of some of the following: Mountain Posture (*page 46*), Prayer Pose (*page 44*), The Tree (*page 44*), Chest Expander (*page 47*), Stick Posture (*page 48*), Legs Up (*page 50*), Pose of a Child (*page 55*), Half Shoulderstand (*page 62*), Full Shoulderstand (*page 63*), Candle Concentration (*page 71*), Palming (*page 71*). Alternate Nostril Breathing (*page 73*).

Daily practice should also include the Pose of Tranquillity (*page 51*), or The Crocodile (*page 52*), and any of the following breathing exercises: Anti-Anxiety Breath, Cleansing (Dynamic or Simple), Complete Breath, Humming Breath, Sighing Breath. Eye exercises, Eye Splashing.

Nutrients

Vitamin A, carotenes, the B vitamins (particularly B_1, B_5, B_6, B_9, B_{12}, B_{15}, biotin, PABA), anti-stress factors, vitamins C, E, EFAs, calcium, copper, iodine, iron, magnesium, manganese, potassium, phosphorus, selenium, silicon, zinc.

FITS

(*see Epilepsy*)

FLATULENCE

Flatulence is excessive gas in the stomach and intestines, which may result in belching, bloating and abdominal pain.

Gas is generally regarded as a symptom of a minor digestive disorder. In older adults, intestinal gas is likely to be because of a deficiency of enzymes needed to help digest carbohydrates in milk, fruit or vegetables. Dental defects, such as missing teeth or poorly fitting dentures, may result in improper chewing of food and swallowing of air. Gas may also be a symptom of lactose intolerance, a digestive disorder in which the enzyme that breaks down milk sugar is lacking.

Exercises

Squatting Posture (*page 39*), Rock-and-Roll (*page 36*), Supine Knee Squeeze (*page 49*), Pose of Tranquillity (*page 51*), The Crocodile (*page 52*), Pose of a Child (*page 55*), The Cobra (*page 57*), Half Locust (*page 58*). Perineal Exercise. Anti-Anxiety Breath, Breathing Away Pain (for pain relief), Cleansing Breath (Dynamic), Complete Breath.

Nutrients

The B vitamins (particularly B_1, B_3, B_5), vitamin K, potassium.

GALL BLADDER DISEASE

(*see also Jaundice*)

The gall bladder is a small pouch located under the liver, and its ducts can be the site of cancerous or non-cancerous tumours, gall stones and inflammations caused by infection or chemical irritation.

Exercises

Mountain Posture (*page 40*), Angle Balance (*page 42*), Supine Knee Squeeze (*page 49*), Pose of Tranquillity (*page 51*), The Crocodile (*page 52*), Pose of a Child (*page 55*), The Cobra (*page 57*), Half Locust (*page 58*), Half Moon (*page 66*), Spinal Twist (*page 61*), Half Shoulderstand (*page 62*), Full Shoulderstand (*page 63*). Alternate Nostril Breathing (*page 73*). Anti-Anxiety Breath, Breathing Away Pain (for pain relief), Cleansing Breath (Simple), Complete Breath.

Nutrients

Vitamin A, the B vitamins (particularly B_3, B_6, B_9), anti-stress factors, vitamins C, D, E, EFAs, vitamin K, calcium, magnesium, zinc, dietary fibre, lecithin.

GAS

(*see Flatulence*)

GASTRIC ULCER

(*see Ulcers*)

GASTRITIS

(*see Stomach Disorders*)

GOITRE

(*see Thyroid Gland Problems*)

GOUT

(*see Arthritis*)

HAEMORRHOIDS (PILES)

(*see also Varicose Veins*)

Haemorrhoids are inflamed and locally dilated varicose veins of the rectum or anus, which can be either external or internal. They may be caused by chronic constipation, and can be painful during defaecation where bleeding sometimes occurs.

Yoga can help prevent piles by improving circulation to the anus and by reducing constipation.

Exercises

The Butterfly (*page 34*), Squatting posture (*page 39*), Angle Balance (*page 42*), Abdominal Lift (*page 47*), Legs Up (*page 50*), Pose of Tranquillity (*page 51*), The Crocodile (*page 52*), The Plough (*page 54*), Pose of a Child (*page 55*), The Cobra (*page 57*), Lying Twist (*page 35*), Half Shoulderstand (*page 62*), Full Shoulderstand (*page 63*). Alternate Nostril Breathing (*page 73*). Anti-Anxiety Breath, Breathing Away Pain (for pain relief), Cleansing Breath (Simple), Complete Breath. Perineal Exercise and Sitz Bath. *Note. Consult your doctor* before exercising. *Do not* practise these or other exercises (except for the gentler breathing and relaxation exercises) if you have recently-formed blood clots.

Nutrients

Vitamin A, the B vitamins (particularly B_6), vitamin C, flavonoids, vitamin E, EFAs, calcium, copper, manganese, potassium, zinc, dietary fibre, lecithin. Drink plenty of water.

HAIR LOSS

(*see Alopecia*)

HAY FEVER

(*see Allergies*)

HEADACHE

(*see also Eyestrain, Pain, Sinusitis and Stress*)

Headaches are usually a symptom of another disorder and can be caused by almost any disturbance.

Transient acute headaches may have a variety of causes, including: diseases of the nasal sinuses, teeth, eyes, ears, nose or throat; acute infections; or trauma to the head. Chronic headaches may occur as a result of a variety of conditions, such as stress, fevers, metabolic disorders or exposure to toxic chemicals.

Cluster headache is a headache similar to migraine, recurring as often as two or three times a day over a period of weeks. It tends to strike men between the ages of 40 to 60, and is thought to occur because of a blood vessel disorder. Cluster headaches usually come on abruptly and are characterized by intense throbbing on one side of the head, and pain behind the nostril and one eye. The eyes and nose also water and the skin becomes flushed.

Migraine is a sudden attack of headache, often on one side, usually accompanied by disordered vision, upset stomach and intestines, and sometimes sweating. Attacks may occur from several times a week to several times a year.

The cause of migraine is really unknown but is thought by some to be a blood vessel disorder. There is also a family history of the condition in more than half the sufferers.

Sinus headache involves a frontal sinus (in the forehead, over the eyes), and is best relieved by keeping the head upright. A headache caused by a problem in the maxillary sinus (in the cheekbones, below the eyes) usually improves by lying down.

Tension headache (muscle-contraction headache) is associated with chronic contraction of the neck and scalp muscles and with emotional or physical strain.

Vascular headaches or 'sick' headaches send a throbbing pain into one or both sides of the head during an attack. They are caused by an inflammation of blood vessel walls. Migraine is the most common form of this type of headache.

Other causes of headache include: poor postural habits, eyestrain, TMJ syndrome, low blood sugar (hypoglycaemia), fever, lack of oxygen, caffeine withdrawal and hangover. A severe headache in an older adult, particularly if it begins suddenly, may also be a sign of a serious condition, such as high blood pressure, stroke, glaucoma or brain tumour.

Yoga provides an effective alternative to painkillers through exercises that reduce the build up of tension and promote calm. It helps prevent the vicious circle of fear—tension—pain, and in time, with regular practice, you may require less medication as the frequency, intensity and duration of headaches lessen. Before decreasing medication dosages, however, please *check with your doctor.* (If you suspect that food allergies may be contributing to your headache, pleased have this looked into by a qualified health professional.)

Exercises

Neck exercises performed very slowly and carefully (Chapter 5). The Lion (*page 43*), Legs Up (*page 50*), Pose of Tranquillity (*page 51*), The Crocodile (*page 52*), Candle Concentration (*page 71*), Palming (*page 71*). Alternate Nostril Breathing (*page 73*). Anti-Anxiety Breath. Modify the Breathing Away

Pain exercise as follows: focus attention on your hands and, with each exhalation, visualize them becoming warm (this somehow improves blood flow in the head). Meditation.

Nutrients

Vitamin A, the B vitamins (particularly B_1, B_3, B_5, B_6, B_{12}, choline, PABA), vitamins C, E, EFAs, calcium, iron, magnesium, potassium.

HEARTBURN

(*see Stomach Disorders*)

HEART DISEASE

(*see also Angina Pectoris, Diabetes Mellitus, Blood Pressure and Obesity*)

Heart disease is a general term used to describe any pathological condition of the heart.

The most common cause of death among adults in industrialized societies is coronary heart disease resulting from atherosclerosis, which is a gradual build-up of fatty deposits (mainly cholesterol) on the inner lining of artery walls. It progressively narrows the arteries and decreases the blood flow through them. As blood flow is diminished, the heart muscle supplied by these arteries receives less oxygen and nutrients. Consequently, the heart muscle's ability to pump blood is increasingly threatened.

The process of atherosclerosis may begin as early as 20 years of age. Decreasing risk factors may help slow down the process. These risk factors include cigarette smoking, being overweight, lack of regular exercise, a high-fat diet and stress.

Yogic relaxation and other practices help

you to develop the self-discipline you need to reduce risk factors.

Exercises

Mountain Posture (*page 40*), Stick Posture (*page 48*), Pose of Tranquillity (*page 51*), Candle Concentration (*page 71*), Palming (*page 71*). Alternate Nostril Breathing (*page 73*). Anti-Anxiety Breath, Cleansing Breath (Simple), Complete Breath, Sighing Breath (if the chest feels tight), Humming Breath. Meditation.

Nutrients

Vitamin A, the B vitamins (particularly B_1, B_3, B_5, B_6, B_9, B_{15}, choline inositol), anti-stress factors, vitamins C, D, E, EFAs, calcium, chromium, copper, iodine, magnesium, molybdenum, potassium, selenium, vanadium, zinc, carnitine, lecithin.

HERNIA (RUPTURE)

A hernia is the protrusion or projection of an organ, or part of an organ, through the wall of the cavity that normally encloses it.

Causes of herniae include: structural weakness from debilitating illness; pressure from a tumour; injury; pregnancy; being overweight; and increased pressure within the abdomen from lifting heavy loads, or even from coughing.

Abdominal hernia is a hernia through the abdominal wall.

Hiatus (diaphragmatic) hernia refers to protrusion of the stomach through the diaphragm – the muscular wall that separates the abdomen from the chest.

Inguinal hernia is the protrusion of the intestine into the groin, which occurs most commonly among men.

Umbilical hernia describes a hernia occurring at the navel, which is more frequent in women than in men.

Exercises

Mountain Posture (*page 40*), Angle Balance (*page 42*), Prayer Pose (*page 44*), Stick Posture (*page 48*), Pose of Tranquillity (*page 51*), Triangle Posture (*page 55*), Angle Posture (*page 61*). Alternate Nostril Breathing (*page 73*). Cleansing Breath (Simple), Complete Breath.

Nutrients

Vitamin E, EFAs, magnesium, potassium. Adequate protein intake.

HIGH BLOOD PRESSURE

(*see Blood Pressure*)

HOT FLUSHES

(*see Menopausal Symptoms*)

HYPERTENSION

(*see Blood Pressure*)

HYPERVENTILATION

(*see also Anxiety and Panic Attack*)

Hyperventilation is abnormally deep and rapid breathing, which results in a depletion of carbon dioxide in the blood. Symptoms include: a fall in blood pressure; occasional fainting; increased anxiety; tingling of the arms and legs; headache and blurred vision.

Causes of hyperventilation cover nervous system disorders, oxygen depletion, low blood sugar or exposure to toxic chemicals. The condition may also be caused by an emotional disorder such as anxiety.

For immediate treatment, get the person who is hyperventilating to breathe into a paper bag until the carbon dioxide content of the blood has had a chance to return to normal. Reassure the person and try to calm him/her by patiently instructing, step by step, in a technique designed to slow down the breathing, such as the Anti-Anxiety Breath.

Exercises

Pose of Tranquillity (*page 51*). Alternate Nostril Breathing (*page 73*). Anti-Anxiety Breath, Cleansing Breath (Simple), Complete Breath, Whispering Breath.

Nutrients

The B vitamins (particularly B_1, B_3, B_6, biotin), anti-stress factors, EFAs (omega-3 fatty acids), calcium, magnesium, potassium.

(IBS) IRRITABLE BOWEL SYNDROME

(*see also Anxiety, Inflammatory Bowel Disease and Stress*)

While the symptoms of IBS often resemble those of inflammatory bowel disease, the bowel is not inflamed.

IBS is the most common disorder of the gastrointestinal tract in industrialized societies. It usually occurs in the middle years of life, developing more often in women than in men. Its key features are abdominal discomfort or pain, accompanied by diarrhoea and/or constipation. There is no known physical cause.

Movement through the bowel is controlled by the autonomic nervous system, under the influence of the hypothalamus (neural control system) in the brain. Bowel action can, therefore, be affected by your mental state – in fact, many bowel disorders are a result of stress.

Exercise is a necessary part of the treatment for IBS. By directly affecting intestinal motility, exercise can help to reduce constipation. Since exercise also reduces anxiety, it can be therapeutic in cases where IBS is stress related. Yoga breathing, relaxation and meditation practices are superb for helping you control anxiety and deal effectively with stress.

Note. Food sensitivities may contribute to symptoms. Please consult a qualified health professional to help identify any food allergies you may have.

Exercises

Mountain Posture (*page 40*), Angle Balance (*page 42*), Stick Posture (*page 48*), Supine Knee Squeeze (*page 49*), Pose of Tranquillity (*page 51*), The Crocodile (*page 52*), Pose of a Child (*page 55*), The Cobra (*page 57*), Half Moon (*page 60*), Spinal Twist (*page 61*), Half Shoulderstand (*page 62*), Full Shoulderstand (*page 63*), Sun Salutations (*pages 65–68*), Candle Concentration (*page 71*). Alternate Nostril Breathing (*page 73*). Anti-Anxiety Breath, Breathing Away Pain (for pain relief), Cleansing Breath (Simple), Complete Breath, Humming Breath. Meditation. Perineal Exercise and Sitz Bath as necessary.

Nutrients

Vitamin A, carotenes, the B vitamins (particularly B_1, B_9, PABA), anti-stress factors, vitamins C, D, E, EFAs (omega-3 fatty acids), calcium, fluoride, iron, magnesium, potassium, selenium, zinc. Adequate complex carbohydrate intake.

IMMUNE SYSTEM DISORDERS

(*see also AIDS, Allergies, Arthritis, Autoimmune Disorders and Cancer*)

Your immune system is part of your body's natural protection against environmental threats such as pollutants and microorganisms. The system consists of five types of white blood cells, bone marrow, the thymus gland, the lymphatic glands, the spleen, tonsils, adenoids and the appendix.

One of the characteristics of a properly functioning immune system is its ability to recognize a foreign agent that has entered the body and to protect the body from being harmed. Sometimes, however, the system fails.

In *autoimmune diseases* the body seemingly wages war against itself.

Some medical researchers believe that *rheumatoid arthritis* is a consequence of an attack on the joints by the body's immune system.

Multiple (disseminated) *sclerosis*, or MS, is the most common nervous system disease affecting young adults. It is also classified as an autoimmune disease.

Systemic Lupus Erythematosus (SLE or Lupus) us yet another autoimmune disorder. It is a complex syndrome which can affect many tissues and organs, including: the heart and blood vessels, lungs, kidneys, brain and nervous system, joints, skin and collagen (a fibrous insoluble protein found in connective tissue).

Inappropriate or excessive activations of the immune system are generally referred to as *allergies* – technically as *hypersensitivity reactions.*

AIDS severely damages the immune system, making the body vulnerable to many other illnesses including pneumonia and cancer. There also appears to be a higher incidence of *cancer* among people with a suppressed immune system than among the general population.

Exercises

Warm-ups (*pages 33–36*), The Tree (*page 44*), Pose of Tranquillity (*page 51*), The Crocodile (*page 52*), The Plough (*page 54*), Angle Posture (*page 61*), Spinal Twist (*page 61*), Half Shoulderstand (*page 62*), Full Shoulderstand (*page 63*), Sun Salutations (*pages 65–68*). Alternate Nostril Breathing (*page 73*). Any of the breathing and meditative exercises. Nasal Wash.

Nutrients

Vitamin A, carotenes, the B vitamins (particularly B_2, B_3, B_5, B_6, B_9, B_{12}, B_{15}), anti-stress factors, vitamin C, flavonoids, vitamins D, E, EFAs, calcium, copper, iron, manganese, molybdenum, selenium, vanadium, zinc, carnitine.

IMPOTENCE

(*see Sexual Problems*)

INCONTINENCE (OF URINE)

This is an involuntary inability to retain urine, usually because of a loss of control of the sphincter muscles which open and close the urethra. It may be caused by various conditions, including a disease or injury involving the brain or spinal cord.

Stress-related incontinence of urine is leakage of small amounts of urine during coughing, laughing or sneezing. It results from increased pressure within the abdomen, in a person with weak sphincter muscles.

Urinary incontinence tends to increase with age and is somewhat more common in women than in men. A weakening of pelvic tissues from childbearing is one cause for this, while in older women, the condition may involve a decreased level of the hormone oestrogen. In men, an enlarged prostate gland may be a causal factor, as may be a weakness of genito-urinary structures (referring to the genitals and urinary organs) following surgery on the prostate gland.

Exercises

The Butterfly (*page 34*), Squatting Posture (*page 39*), Knee and Thigh Stretch (*page 39*), Pose of Tranquillity (*page 51*), Star Posture (*page 53*), Spread Leg Stretch (*page 54*), Pelvic Stretch (*page 56*), The Camel (*page 56*), Lying Twist (*page 35*), Side Leg Raise (*page 59*), Spinal Twist (*page 61*), Half Shoulderstand (*page 62*), Full Shoulderstand (*page 63*). Alternate Nostril Breathing (*page 73*). Anti-Anxiety Breath, Cleansing Breath (Simple), Complete Breath. Meditation, Perineal Exercise and Sitz Bath.

Nutrients

Vitamin A, the B vitamins, (particularly B_6), anti-stress factors, vitamins C, E, EFAs (omega-3 fatty acids), calcium, magnesium, potassium, zinc.

INDIGESTION

(*see Stomach Disorders*)

INFLAMMATORY BOWEL DISEASE

(see also Anxiety, Irritable Bowel Syndrome and Stress)

There are two major forms of chronic inflammatory disease of the intestines: Crohn's disease and ulcerative colitis.

Crohn's disease (regional enteritis) is often found in the lower part of the small intestine (ileum), but may occur in the colon (large intestine). It commonly progresses to involve all layers of the intestinal wall.

Ulcerative colitis is a disease in which ulcers develop in the lining of the colon. Please *consult your doctor immediately* if you suspect you may have either disorder.

Both diseases produce abdominal pain and diarrhoea which, in ulcerative colitis, is usually bloody. (Irritable bowel syndrome, while it may cause abdominal pain and diarrhoea, is not an inflammatory disease.)

Depending on the severity of the disorder, people with inflammatory bowel disease may become seriously malnourished because of poor absorption of nutrients from the intestines into the blood stream. It is, therefore, very important to have your nutritional status monitored by your doctor (or other therapist), to ensure that your basic needs for protein and energy are being met; also to determine whether you have developed any of the numerous nutritional deficiencies that may arise during the course of the disease.

Please consider consulting a qualified health professional to help identify any food sensitivities you may have.

Exercises

Angle Balance (*page 42*), Supine Knee Squeeze (*page 49*), Pose of Tranquillity (*page 51*), The Crocodile (*page 52*), Pose of a Child (*page 55*), Half Shoulderstand (*page 62*), Full Shoulderstand (*page 63*), Candle Concentration (*page 71*). Alternate Nostril Breathing (*page 73*). Anti-Anxiety Breath, Breathing Away Pain (for pain relief), Cleansing Breath (Simple), Complete Breath, Humming Breath. Meditation.

Nutrients

Vitamin A, carotenes, the B vitamins (particularly B_9), anti-stress factors, vitamins C, D, E, F, K, EFAs (omega-3 fatty acids), calcium, fluoride, iron, magnesium, potassium, selenium, zinc. Adequate complex carbohydrate intake.

INFLUENZA

(see also Colds)

Flu is an acute contagious respiratory infection characterized by sudden onset, fever, chills, headache, general malaise and muscle pain. Sore throat, cough and cold symptoms are also common. The causative agent is a virus of which several species have been identified.

Particularly vulnerable to flu are older people with an immune system weakened by other diseases or poor nutrition.

Exercises

Mountain Posture (*page 40*), The Lion (*page 43*) (for a sore throat), Chest Expander (*page 47*), Fish Posture (*page 49*), Pose of Tranquillity (*page 51*), The Crocodile (*page 52*). Alternate Nostril Breathing (*page 73*). All the breathing exercises are appropriate. Nasal Wash.

Nutrients

Vitamin A, carotenes, the B vitamins, anti-stress factors, vitamin C, flavonoids, vitamins D, E, EFAs, calcium, copper, iron, magnesium, potassium, selenium, zinc.

INSOMNIA

(*see also Anxiety, Depression and Pain*)

The condition insomnia applies to both an inability to sleep, and to sleep prematurely ended or interrupted by periods of wakefulness.

Sleep patterns change as people grow older, and periods of sleep, as well as total sleeping time, tend to become shorter than in younger years. This is normal and does not in itself represent a change in one's health.

Isomnia is not a disease but may be the symptom of disease. The most frequent causes are anxiety, depression and pain.

Exercises

Mountain Posture (*page 40*), Pose of Tranquillity (*page 51*), The Crocodile (*page 52*), Back-stretching Posture (*page 53*), The Cobra (*page 57*), Spinal Twist (*page 61*), the Sun Salutations (*pages 65–68*). Anti-Anxiety Breath, Cleansing Breath (Simple), Complete Breath, Humming Breath. Meditation.

Nutrients

The B vitamins (particularly B_1, B_3, B_5, B_6, biotin, choline), anti-stress factors, calcium, magnesium, potassium.

INTERMITTENT CLAUDICATION

(*see also Angina Pectoris and Cramp*)

Intermittent claudication is a severe pain in the calf muscle, which occurs during walking or exertion, but subsides with rest. It causes lameness or limping, and results from inadequate blood supply to the leg muscles – possibly because of arterial spasms, atherosclerosis or a similar condition.

The cause and effect of intermittent claudication are similar to those of the condition that causes angina pectoris. Insufficient blood flow to the leg muscles causes oxygen starvation of the tissues, resulting in painful leg cramps that often restrict walking. After a few minutes of rest the symptoms disappear and walking can be resumed.

Exercises

To improve circulation and prevent leg cramps, regularly practise: Ankle Rotation (Chapter 5), Rock-and-Roll (*page 36*), Legs Up (*page 50*), Pose of Tranquillity (*page 50*), Half Shoulderstand (*page 62*), Full Shoulderstand (*page 63*), Dog Stretch (*page 64*), Sun Salutations (*pages 65–68*). Alternate Nostril Breathing (*page 73*). Anti-Anxiety Breath, Breathing Away Pain (to relieve cramp), Cleansing Breath (Simple), Sighing Breath. Meditation.

Nutrients

Vitamin A, the B vitamins (particularly B_1, B_2, B_3, B_5, B_6, biotin, choline, inositol), anti-stress factors, vitamins C, D, E, EFAs, calcium, magnesium, potassium, selenium, zinc, carnitine, lecithin.

ITCHING (PRURITUS)

(*see also Anxiety and Stress*)

Pruritis may be a symptom of a disease process such as an allergic response, or it may arise because of emotional factors.

Exercises

The Tree (*page 44*), Balance Posture (*page 45*), Pose of Tranquillity (*page 51*), The Crocodile (*page 52*), Half Shoulderstand (*page 62*), Full Shoulderstand (*page 63*), Candle Concentration (*page 71*). Alternate Nostril Breathing (*page 73*). Anti-Anxiety Breath, Cleansing Breath (Dynamic and Simple), Complete Breath, Cooling Breath, Humming Breath. Meditation.

Nutrients

Vitamin A, the B vitamins (particularly B_2, B_5, B_6), anti-stress factors, vitamins C, E, EFAs, calcium, magnesium.

JAUNDICE

(*see also Gall Bladder Disease*)

Jaundice is a condition characterized by yellowness of the skin, whites of the eyes, mucous membranes and body fluids. It may be caused by the destruction of bile passageways, excess destruction of red blood cells or liver disturbances.

Jaundice may simply indicate a benign and curable disease such as gall-stones, but may also indicate disease of the liver or gall bladder, or cancer of the pancreas involving the bile duct.

Exercises

Mountain Posture (*page 40*), Angle Balance (*page 42*), Supine Knee Squeeze (*page 49*), Pose of Tranquillity (*page 51*), The Crocodile (*page 52*), Pose of a Child (*page 55*), The Cobra (*page 57*), Half Locust (*page 58*), Half Moon (*page 60*), Spinal Twist (*page 61*), Half Shoulderstand (*page 62*), Full Shoulderstand (*page 63*). Alternate Nostril Breathing (*page 73*). Anti-Anxiety Breath, Breathing Away Pain (for pain relief), Cleansing Breath (Simple), Complete Breath.

Nutrients

Vitamin A, the B vitamins (particularly B_1, B_2, B_3, B_5, B_6, B_9, B_{15}, choline), anti-stress factors, vitamin C, D, E, calcium, magnesium, zinc, dietary fibre, lecithin.

JOINT DISORDERS

(*see also Arthritis and Pain*)

Degenerative and other diseases affecting the tissues of the hands, feet, hips, knees, spine and other areas normally cushioned with cartilage all fall into this category.

Osteoarthritis (OA) is the most common joint disorder, and is caused by 'wear and tear' on the cartilage surfaces of joints.

Factors that aggravate symptoms of OA are being overweight, poor posture, injury and repetitive work patterns (for example, construction workers tend to develop OA of the elbow and shoulder joints).

Exercises

Warm-up exercises, Squatting Posture (*page 39*), Cow Head Posture (*page 41*), Prayer Pose (*page 44*), Eagle Posture (*page 46*), Chest

Expander (*page 47*), Stick Posture (*page 48*), Pose of Tranquillity (*page 51*), The Crocodile (*page 52*), Back-stretching Posture (*page 53*), The Plough (*page 54*), Triangle Posture (*page 55*), The Cobra (*page 57*), Lying Twist (*page 35*), Angle Posture (*page 61*), Spinal Twist (*page 61*), Sun Salutations (*pages 65–68*), Cat Stretch series (*pages 69–70*). Alternate Nostril Breathing (*page 73*). Anti-Anxiety Breath, Cleansing Breath (Dynamic and Simple), Complete Breath. Meditation.

Nutrients

Vitamins C, D, calcium, copper, fluoride, manganese, silicon, zinc.

KIDNEY DISORDERS

(*see also Blood Pressure, High*)

Inflammation of the kidneys (nephritis), kidney stones and kidney failure are only three of the many conditions that can result when the kidneys are affected.

Symptoms of kidney disorder include pain, fever, swelling (oedema) and disturbances in the passing of urine and occasionally blood in the urine.

Kidney stones (renal calculi) are increasingly common in industrialized countries. People prone to kidney stone formation should minimize, or avoid altogether, the consumption of animal protein, and decrease their intake of fat, refined sugar, salt, alcohol and caffeine. On the other hand, they should increase their intake of dietary fibre and fluids, and drink hard water in preference to soft.

Exercises

The Butterfly (*page 34*), Knee and Thigh Stretch (*page 39*), Rock-and-Roll (*page 36*),

Supine Knee Squeeze (*page 49*), Pose of Tranquillity (*page 51*), Back-stretching Posture (*page 53*), Spread Leg Stretch (*page 54*), The Plough (*page 54*), Pelvic Stretch (*page 56*), The Camel (*page 56*), The Cobra (*page 57*), Half Locust (*page 58*), The Bow (*page 59*), Side Leg Raise (*page 59*), Spinal Twist (*page 61*). Also Half Shoulderstand (*page 62*), Full Shoulderstand (*page 63*) and Sun Salutations (*pages 65–68*) (*omit if you have high blood pressure*). Alternate Nostril Breathing (*page 73*). Anti-Anxiety Breath, Breathing Away Pain, Cleansing Breath (Simple), Complete Breath, Humming Breath.

Nutrients

Vitamin A, the B vitamins (particularly B_2, B_5, B_6, B_9, B_{12}, choline), anti-stress factors, vitamin C, flavonoids, vitamins D, E, EFAs (omega-3 fatty acids), calcium, copper, iron, magnesium, potassium, zinc, dietary fibre, lecithin. Drink plenty of water.

LASSITUDE

(*see Fatigue*)

LIVER DISORDERS

(*see also Jaundice*)

The liver is responsible for most of the body's chemical activities, including: the metabolism of proteins, fats and carbohydrates; the regulation of blood sugar' the processing of blood components; the manufacture of bile; and the converting of poisonous substances into less harmful material which can be excreted from the body.

It is not surprising, therefore, that liver disorders can affect healthy body function in a variety of ways to produce a wide range of symptoms. These include: fever, general malaise, appetite loss, weight loss, pain, anaemia, abdominal swelling and jaundice.

Cancer of the liver may be caused by some industrial chemicals, nutritional deficiencies, and as a consequence of cirrhosis of the liver.

Cirrhosis of the liver is a disease marked by the formation of fibrous tissue and nodules in the liver. The causes cover excessive use of alcohol, viral infection, some medications and industrial chemicals.

Hepatitis (inflammation of the liver) is usually manifested by jaundice and, in some cases, by liver enlargement. Symptoms include headache, fever, stomach and intestinal upsets, appetite loss and itching – depending on the particular type of hepatitis. Exposure to certain poisons and viral agents is among the causes of hepatitis.

Exercises

Japanese Sitting Position (*page 38*), Mountain Posture (*page 40*), Angle Balance (*page 42*), Chest Expander (*page 47*), Stick Posture (*page 48*), Supine Knee Squeeze (*page 49*), Pose of Tranquillity (*page 51*), The Crocodile (*page 52*), Pose of a Child (*page 55*), Pelvic Stretch (*page 56*), The Camel (*page 56*), The Cobra (*page 57*), Half Locust (*page 58*), The Bow (*page 59*), Lying Twist (*page 35*), Spinal Twist (*page 61*), Half Shoulderstand (*page 62*), Full Shoulderstand (*page 63*), Sun Salutations (*pages 65–68*). Alternate Nostril Breathing (*page 73*). Anti-Anxiety Breath, Cleansing Breath (Dynamic and Simple), Complete Breath. Meditation.

Nutrients

Vitamin A, the B vitamins (particularly B_1, B_2, B_3, B_5, B_6, B_9, B_{15}, choline), anti-stress factors, vitamins C, E, calcium, iodine, magnesium, dietary fibre, lecithin.

LUMBAGO

(*see Backache*)

LUNG DISORDERS

(*see Breathing Problems*)

LUPUS (SLE)

(*see Autoimmune Disorders and Immune System Disorders*)

ME (MYALGIC ENCEPHALOMYELITIS)

(*see also Depression and Fatigue*)

Myalgic refers to muscle pain; *encephalo* indicates brain; *myelo* pertains to the spinal cord; and *itis* means inflammation. ME is thus an illness that affects the brain, muscles and nervous system, causing pain and inflammation. It is known in the United States as *Chronic Fatigue Syndrome* (CFS).

The most striking symptom of ME is severe, chronic incapacitating fatigue. For a diagnosis of ME to be made, however, the fatigue must have persisted for six months, accompanied by other symptoms including: aching muscles and joints, headache, sore throat, painful lymph nodes, fever, muscle weakness, sleep disturbance, mental fatigue, difficulty in concentrating and mood swings.

There is still controversy over the cause(s) of ME, but research in Britain and Canada has focused on the role of enteroviruses as a primary contributing factor.

ME can occur at any age, but is most common in young and middle-aged persons, particularly women.

Exercises

Your exercise programme should be planned to gradually build up energy reserves. Start with gentle warm-ups and short walks. As your energy increases, add to your exercise regime the Sun Salutations (*pages 65–68*) performed slowly. Also suggested is the daily practice of: Prayer Pose (*page 44*), Pose of Tranquillity (*page 51*), The Crocodile (*page 52*), Half Moon (*page 60*), Spinal Twist (*page 61*), Half Shoulderstand (*page 62*) and/or Full Shoulderstand (*page 63*) (as energy permits), Palming (*page 71*). Alternate Nostril Breathing (*page 73*). Anti-Anxiety Breath, Breathing Away Pain (modified to 'breathe away fatigue'), Cleansing Breath (Simple), Complete Breath. Eye exercises.

Nutrients

Vitamin A, carotenes, the B vitamins, anti-stress factors, vitamin C, flavonoids, vitamin E, EFAs, calcium, copper, iodine, iron, magnesium, manganese, phosphorus, potassium, selenium, silicon, zinc.

MELANCHOLIA

(*see Depression*)

MEMORY, IMPAIRED

Memory has been described as the mental registration, retention and recall of past experience, knowledge, ideas, sensations and thoughts. Registration of experience is favoured by clear comprehension during intense consciousness. Retention of memory differs greatly from one individual to another.

Various memory defects occur in many disorders such as psychoses, organic brain disease and malnutrition, and as a side-effect of drugs or the result of alcohol abuse. Some types of memory loss which are temporary or reversible include those associated with epileptic seizures, head injury, malnutrition, low blood sugar or diseases such as hypothyroidism (underactive thyroid gland).

Yoga practices are particularly useful for memory deficits resulting from fatigue or poor concentration.

Exercises

Mountain Posture (*page 40*), Angle Balance (*page 42*), The Tree (*page 44*), Balance Posture (*page 45*), Eagle Posture (*page 46*), Chest Expander (*page 47*), Stick Posture (*page 48*), Pose of Tranquillity (*page 51*), The Crocodile (*page 52*), The Plough (*page 54*), The Cobra (*page 57*), Spinal Twist (*page 61*), Half Shoulderstand (*page 62*), Full Shoulderstand (*page 63*), Mock Headstand (*page 64*), Dog Stretch (*page 64*), Sun Salutations (*pages 65–68*), Candle Concentration (*page 71*), Palming (*page 71*). Alternate Nostril Breathing (*page 73*). Anti-Anxiety Breath, Cleansing Breath (Simple), Complete Breath, Humming Breath. Meditation.

Nutrients

The B vitamins (particularly B_1, B_3, B_5, B_6, B_{12}, biotin, choline), anti-stress factors, vitamins C, E, calcium, iodine, magnesium, manganese, potassium, zinc, carnitine.

MENOPAUSAL SYMPTOMS

(see also Osteoporosis)

Menopause is that period which marks the permanent cessation of menstrual activity. It usually occurs between the ages of 35 and 58 years. Menstruation may stop suddenly; there may be a decreased flow each month until final cessation; or the interval between periods may be lengthened until menstrual activity stops altogether. Menopause can occur as a result of surgical removal of the ovaries.

Symptoms associated with menopause include: hot flushes (or flashes); nervousness; excessive perspiration; chills; mood swings, low energy and fatigue; depression; crying as a result of circumstances that would not normally produce that reaction; insomnia; heart palpitation; dizziness; headache; urinary disturbances; vaginal irritation; and various stomach and intestinal upsets. Many of these symptoms are thought to arise because of a decline in oestrogen production.

Since oestrogen provides some protection against bone loss, myocardial infarction (heart attack), stroke and hardening of the arteries (arteriosclerosis), postmenopausal women are more vulnerable to these conditions (as well as osteoporosis) than women who are still menstruating regularly.

The use of oestrogen as a 'cure-all'; for menopausal symptoms has been seriously questioned because of undesirable side effects and a link to cancer. Many doctors suggest a yearly pelvic examination, including a Pap test (Papanicolaod test) for detecting cervical cancer.

Exercises

The Butterfly (*page 34*), Knee and Thigh Stretch (*page 39*), Mountain Posture (*page 40*), Angle Balance (*page 42*), The Tree (*page 44*), Balance Posture (*page 45*), Chest Expander (*page 47*), Abdominal Lift (*page 47*), Rock-and-Roll (*page 36*), Fish Posture (*page 49*), Pose of Tranquillity (*page 51*), Back-stretching Posture (*page 53*), Star Posture (*page 53*), Spread Leg Stretch (*page 54*), The Plough (*page 54*), Pelvic Stretch (*page 56*), The Camel (*page 56*), The Cobra (*page 57*), The Bow (*page 59*), Lying Twist (*page 35*), Side Leg Raise (*page 59*), Spinal Twist (*page 61*), Sun Salutations (*pages 65–68*). Alternate Nostril Breathing (*page 73*). Anti-Anxiety Breath, Cleansing Breath (Dynamic), Complete Breath. Meditation. Perineal Exercise.

Nutrients

Vitamin A, the B vitamins (particularly B_5, B_6), anti-stress factors, vitamin C, flavonoids, vitamins D, E, EFAs (omega-6 fatty acids), calcium, iodine, iron, magnesium, selenium, zinc.

MENSTRUAL IRREGULARITIES AND PMS

(see also Pelvic Inflammatory Disease)

Premenstrual Syndrome (PMS) is a group of signs and symptoms occurring several days prior to the onset of menstruation. The condition is characterized by one or more of the following: irritability; emotional tension; anxiety; mood changes (especially depression); headache; breast tenderness, with or without swelling; and water retention which may cause oedema.

The symptoms of PMS subside close to the onset of menstruation. It is the relief of symptoms by menstruation that distinguishes PMS from dysmenorrhoea.

Dysmenorrhoea is painful menstruation and affects about 50 per cent of menstruating women.

Amenorrhoea is the absence of menstrual flow when it is normally expected.

Menorrhagia is excessive bleeding at the time of a menstrual period, either in number of days and /or amount of blood.

For more information on menstrual irregularities, their causes and treatments, for example, please refer to my book entitled *Pain-Free Periods* (*see the Bibliography for details*).

Exercises

The Butterfly (*page 34*), Squatting Posture (*page 38*), Knee and Thigh Stretch (*page 39*), Mountain Posture (*page 40*), Chest Expander (*page 47*), Supine Knee Squeeze (*page 49*), Fish posture (*page 49*), Legs Up (*page 50*), Pose of Tranquillity (*page 51*), The Crocodile (*page 52*), Star Posture (*page 53*), Spread Leg Stretch (*page 54*), Pose of a Child (*page 55*), Pelvic Stretch (*page 56*), The Camel (*page 56*), Lying Twist (*page 35*), Side Leg Raise (*page 59*), Half Moon (*page 60*), Spinal Twist (*page 61*). When not menstruating the Half Shoulderstand (*page 62*) and Full Shoulderstand (*page 63*). Cat Stretch series (*pages 69–70*). Alternate Nostril Breathing (*page 73*). Anti-Anxiety Breath, Breathing Away Pain (to relieve cramp), Cleansing Breath (Simple), Complete Breath, Humming Breath. Meditation. Perineal Exercise and Sitz bath.

Nutrients

The B vitamins (particularly B_3, B_6, B_9, B_{12}), vitamins C, E, K, EFAs (omega-6 fatty acids), calcium, chromium, iron, magnesium, manganese, zinc.

MIGRAINE

(*see Headache*)

MORNING SICKNESS

(*see Nausea*)

MOTION SICKNESS

(*see Nausea*)

MULTIPLE SCLEROSIS

(*see Immune System Disorders*)

MUSCLE CRAMP

(*see Cramp*)

NAIL CHANGES

Nails protect the end portion of fingers and toes, enhance our sense of touch and enable us to pick up small objects. These functions may be adversely affected by a number of factors including infection, nutritional deficiencies, changes associated with certain skin disorders, tumours and a variety of medical conditions.

For more information on nail changes and what they mean; on nutrition for healthy nails and on all aspects of nail care, please refer to my book entitled *Super Healthy Hair, Skin and Nails* (*see the Bibliography for details*).

Exercises

Mountain Posture (*page 40*), Cow Head Posture (*page 41*), The Flower (*page 42*), Chest

Expander (*page 47*), Pose of Tranquillity (*page 51*), The Crocodile (*page 52*), Pose of a Child (*page 55*), Spinal Twist (*page 61*), Half Shoulderstand (*page 62*), Full Shoulderstand (*page 63*). Alternate Nostril Breathing (*page 73*). Anti-Anxiety Breath, Cleansing Breath (Dynamic), Complete Breath.

Nutrients

Vitamin A, the B vitamins (particularly B_5, B_9), vitamin C, EFAs (omega-6 fatty acids), calcium, iron, silicon, zinc.

NASAL ALLERGY

(*see also Allergies, Breathing Problems and Colds*)

Your nose filters, warms and humidifies the air you breathe in. The sneezing reflex is part of this protective system, as is the swelling of the nasal lining to block the passage of harmful substances, and the secretion of fluid to wash out irritants and prevent them from re-entering the respiratory tract.

Nasal allergy can be triggered by many agents including house dust and pollens, as well as by emotional upsets. It is character-ized by excessive sneezing and a blocked or runny nose.

Yoga practices strengthen the immune system and increase the tolerance of the nasal lining to invading agents. They calm the mind, thus reducing overreactions that precipitate conditions like nasal allergy. The discipline yoga teaches also helps you to give up smoking, which harms the respiratory system.

Exercises

Mountain Posture (*page 40*), Cow Head Posture (*page 41*), Balance Posture (*page 45*),

Chest Expander (*page 47*), Fish Posture (*page 49*), Pose of Tranquillity (*page 51*), The Crocodile (*page 52*), Spinal Twist (*page 61*), Half Shoulderstand (*page 62*), Full Shoulderstand (*page 63*), Dog Stretch (*page 64*), Sun Salutations (*pages 65–68*). Alternate Nostril Breathing (*page 73*). Anti-Anxiety Breath, Cleansing Breath (Dynamic), Complete Breath. Meditation. Nasal Wash.

Nutrients

Vitamin A, carotenes, the B vitamins (particularly B_3, B_5, B_6, B_9, B_{12}, B_{15}), anti-stress factors, vitamin C, flavonoids, vitamins D, E, EFAs, calcium, magnesium, potassium, selenium, zinc.

NAUSEA (FEELING SICK)

Nausea is an unpleasant situation which usually precedes vomiting. It is present in seasickness, often in early pregnancy, in gall bladder disturbances, food poisoning, diseases of the central nervous system and in some emotional states such as anxiety. Nausea is also a side-effect of some drugs, and a symptom of viral infection and exposure to radiation. It may even be brought on by the sight, odour or thought of obnoxious conditions.

Morning sickness refers to the nausea and vomiting which affect some women during the first few months of pregnancy, particularly in the morning. Headache, dizziness and exhaustion may also be experienced. Morning sickness tends to clear up after the third month of pregnancy. In most cases, frequent small snacks of bland foods such as plain biscuits, broths and clear soups bring relief. For more information on morning sickness and other discomforts of pregnancy, together with natural relief measures for them, please refer to my book entitled *Easy Pregnancy with Yoga* (*see the Bibliography for details*).

Motion sickness (travel sickness) occurs when motion affects the middle ear, and the vomiting centre in the brain stem is stimulated. Symptoms of motion sickness include nausea, vomiting and vertigo (dizziness) induced by irregular or rhythmic movements. Headaches may also occur.

Seasickness, airsickness and carsickness are all examples of motion sickness. Try to choose a position in the craft where up-and-down motion is minimized. Avoid dietary and alcoholic excesses, reading or unusual visual stimuli. Lie flat on your back or use a semi-reclining position if you can.

Note. Nausea with vomiting can lead to dehydration. Care should therefore be taken to replace lost fluids.

Exercises

Pose of Tranquillity (*page 51*). Alternate Nostril Breathing (*page 73*). Anti-Anxiety Breath, Cleansing Breath (Simple), Complete Breath, Sighing Breath.

Nutrients

The B vitamins (particularly B_1, B_3, B_5, B_6, B_9, B_{12}, biotin) iron, magnesium, potassium.

NERVOUS DISORDERS

(*see Anxiety, Depression, Insomnia, Panic Attack and Stress*)

NEURASTHENIA

(*see Fatigue*)

NICOTINE ADDICTION

(*see Addiction*)

OBESITY

Obesity means an abnormal amount of fat on the body. The word is used to refer to someone who is from 20 to 30 per cent over the average weight for their age, sex, height and body build.

Obesity is the result of an imbalance between food eaten and energy expended, but the underlying cause is usually complex and the condition difficult to treat. Psychological factors leading to emotional stress, a sedentary lifestyle and social problems are among the contributing causes.

Excess fat plays a role in numerous diseases, particularly among women. These include gall bladder disease, uterine cancer and osteoarthritis. It is also associated with a number of serious disorders including high blood pressure, diabetes and coronary artery disease.

A combination of regular exercise and dietary restriction is the most effective means of losing body fat and maintaining weight loss. Decrease your total calorie intake, increase your intake of dietary fibre, and reduce your fat consumption and sugar and caffeine intake. Seek help in identifying possible food sensitivities.

The discipline inherent in yoga practices will be useful in assisting you to control your eating habits. It will give you control and mastery over mental processes – such as the craving for food as a source of comfort or pleasure – and will help you to resist overindulgence.

Exercises

Mountain Posture (*page 40*), Prayer Pose (*page 44*), Chest Expander (*page 47*), Stick Posture (*page 48*), Pose of Tranquillity (*page 51*), Side Leg Raise (*page 59*), Half Moon (*page 60*), Spinal Twist (*page 61*), Sun Salutations (*pages 65–68*). Alternate Nostril Breathing (*page 73*). Anti-Anxiety Breath, Cleansing Breath (Dynamic), Complete Breath.

Nutrients

Vitamin A, the B vitamins (particularly B_3, B_5, B_6), vitamin C, EFAs (omega-6 fatty acids), iodine, iron, vanadium, carnitine, dietary fibre.

OEDEMA (SWELLING)

A local or generalized condition in which body tissues contain an excessive amount of fluid.

Oedema may result from a wide range of disorders including: heart failure, kidney disease, liver disease, inflammation, malnutrition, infection and injury. It is also a side effect of some drugs.

Oedema often begins insidiously and is first noticed as an unexplained gain in body weight. Eventually it becomes apparent as puffiness in the face or swelling in the legs.

Treatment of the various types of oedema requires correction of the underlying causes. In some cases, salt intake is restricted. Generally, diet should be adequate in protein and calories, and rich in vitamins and minerals (but low in salt).

Pitting oedema usually occurs in the extremities, such as the hands and feet. When the affected area is pressed firmly with a finger, it will maintain the depression produced by the finger. Elevating the swollen limb is often helpful in reducing the swelling.

Exercises

Mountain Posture (*page 40*), Angle Balance (*page 42*), Legs Up (*page 50*), Pose of Tranquillity (*page 51*), Half Locust (*page 58*), Side Leg Raise (*page 59*), Half Shoulderstand (*page 62*), Full Shoulderstand (*page 63*), Sun Salutations (*pages 65–68*). Cleansing Breath (Dynamic), Complete Breath.

Nutrients

Vitamin A, the B vitamins (particularly B_1, B_2, B_3, B_5, B_6, B_9, B_{12}, choline), vitamin C, flavonoids, vitamins D, E, EFAs, calcium, copper, iodine, magnesium, potassium, silicon.

OSTEOARTHRITIS

(*see Arthritis*)

OSTEOPOROSIS

(*see also Menopausal Symptoms*)

Osteoporosis is a bone-loss disorder that affects mainly postmenopausal women and, to a lesser degree, sedentary men. The condition is marked by decreased bone density, as bone breaks down faster than it is being formed. Bone loss takes place in all parts of the skeleton, with the greatest loss tending to occur in spongey bone rather than in compact bone.

Particularly serious are bone losses in the spine and upper leg bone. The spinal bones (vertebrae) become compressed by the weight of the body when weakened by osteoporosis. Compression fractures can reduce a person's height by several centimetres.

The exact cause of loss of bone mass in older adults is unknown, but factors associated with osteoporosis in post-menopausal women include heredity, the amount of bone mass at skeletal maturity, exercise, nutrition and hormonal influences – particularly diminished oestrogen production.

Exercise seems to help in the development of original bone mass and to retard bone mass later in life – it may actually increase bone mass in older women.

The role of nutrition in osteoporosis is related chiefly to the dietary intake of calcium. This tends to be lower in older adults and aggravated by a decreased intestinal absorption than in younger people. Vitamin D availability may also affect calcium absorption.

The part played by the hormone oestrogen is shown by the fact that osteoporosis is rare among women before menopause, but common after menopause.

The use of aluminium-based antacids, alcohol, tobacco and caffeine has also been implicated in lifestyle factors contributing to loss of bone mass.

Oestrogen administration to treat osteoporosis may require special precautions in postmenopausal women who may be vulnerable to cancer. Older men with osteoporosis may be at risk from cancer if they are treated with testosterone.

Exercises

The following postures combined with walking and other weight-bearing exercises. are useful in helping to prevent osteoporosis: Squatting Posture (*page 39*), The Tree (*page 44*), Balance Posture (*page 45*), Eagle Posture (*page 46*), Rock-and-Roll (*page 36*), Back-stretching Posture (*page 53*), The Plough (*page 54*), Triangle Posture (*page 55*), The Cobra (*page 57*), The Bow (*page 59*), Lying Twist (*page 35*), Half Moon (*page 60*), Angle Posture (*page 61*), Spinal Twist (*page 61*), Half Shoulderstand (*page 62*), Full Shoulderstand (*page 63*), Sun Salutations (*pages 65–68*). Alternate Nostril Breathing (*page 73*).

Nutrients

Vitamins C, D, boron, calcium, copper, fluoride, magnesium, manganese, silicon, zinc.

Note. Beware of high-protein diets which leach minerals from the body, including calcium.

OVERBREATHING

(*see Hyperventilation*)

PAIN

(*see also Angina Pectoris, Arthritis, Cramp and Headache*)

Severe pain can produce symptoms of pallor, sweat, 'goose bumps', dilated pupils and an increase in heart rate, blood pressure, breathing and muscle tension.

Pain is considered a protective mechanism which prompts those experiencing it to seek relief and to rectify whatever is causing it. It can be acute, as in the case of an injury, or chronic, as in the case of arthritic conditions.

Medications that counteract pain are called *analgesics*. Used habitually they can sometimes produce unwanted side effects, and some of them are also addictive.

You may wonder why some people seem to

tolerate pain better than others. One plausible explanation is the spinal 'gate control theory' of pain. Simply put, there seems to be a nervous mechanism that, in effect, opens or closes a 'gate' controlling pain stimuli reaching the brain for interpretation. This mechanism can be influenced by certain psychological factors including attitude, anxiety, tension, suggestion and personality. The doctor or other therapist who prescribes only medication for pain relief may be failing to consider such mind-generated factors.

Natural pain control methods, such as yoga practices, are largely based on closing the spinal 'gate'; to influence input from stimuli reaching the brain. Compared with pain management through drugs, these natural methods mobilize the body's natural resources to promote comfort and a sense of well-being.

Yoga recognizes the very close relationship between our respiratory (breathing) system and the perception of and reaction to pain. When we are uncomfortable or in pain, our breathing speeds up and becomes shallow, difficult or irregular. When we are at ease, however, our breathing tends to be slower and more regular.

Yoga breathing techniques teach you how to bring pain under your own conscious, wilful control. They show you how to slow down your breathing to lessen tension and anxiety, and in doing so ease discomfort and pain. They also provide a mental diversion from the pain itself so that it is perceived as less intense. This is one of the principles so successfully used in prenatal classes.

Exercises

People who exercise regularly tend to cope better with pain than those who do not. Regular exercise produces more of the body's natural pain relievers (endorphins and enkephalins).

The following yoga practices are useful in helping you to manage pain effectively: The Tree (*page 44*), Balance Posture (*page 45*), Eagle Posture (*page 46*), Candle Concentration (*page 71*), Alternate Nostril Breathing (*page 73*) (which train you in mental steadiness). Pose of Tranquillity (*page 51*), The Crocodile (*page 52*), Pose of a Child (*page 55*) (which discourage tension build-up and promote relaxation). All the breathing exercises (particularly Breathing Away Pain) are suitable. Meditation.

Nutrients

Vitamin A, the B vitamins (particularly B_1, B_3, B_6, B_9, B_{12}, biotin), anti-stress factors, vitamins C, E, calcium, copper, magnesium, selenium.

PANIC ATTACK

(*see also Anxiety and Hyperventilation*)

A panic attack is an acute attack of anxiety, terror or fright, usually of sudden onset, and which may be uncontrollable enough to require sedation.

Panic attack symptoms include: racing or pounding heartbeat, chest pain, dizziness, lightheadedness, nausea, difficult breathing, tingling or numbness in the hands and dream-like sensations or perceptual distortions.

A panic attack typically lasts for several minutes and is one of the most distressing conditions a person can experience. People who experience repeated panic attacks are said to have a panic disorder. This condition is usually treated with a combination of medication and psychotherapy.

One immediate and effective way to relieve the hyperventilation that accompanies a panic attack is to instruct the individual experiencing it to breathe through one nostril while closing the mouth and the other nostril. Alternatively, instruct the person to breathe into a paper bag.

Exercises

Mountain Posture (*page 40*), The Tree (*page 44*), Balance Posture (*page 45*), Eagle Posture (*page 46*) (to help develop mental steadiness). Chest Expander (*page 47*), Stick Posture (*page 48*), Pose of Tranquillity (*page 51*), The Crocodile (*page 52*). Alternate Nostril Breathing (*page 73*). Anti-Anxiety Breath (also useful during an attack), Cleansing Breath (Simple), Complete Breath, Humming Breath, Whispering Breath. Meditation.

Nutrients

The B vitamins (particularly B_1, B_2, B_6, biotin), anti-stress factors, EFAs, calcium, magnesium.

PERIOD PAIN

(*see Menstrual Irregularities*)

PHOBIAS

(*see also Anxiety and Panic Attack*)

A phobia is a persistent, irrational fear of a specific object, activity or situation which results in a compelling desire to avoid the feared stimulus.

Phobias are classified into three types: agoraphobia (fear of being alone in public places); social phobia and simple phobias.

Exposure to the feared stimulus may cause the individual to panic.

Exercises

(*see Anxiety*)

Nutrients

(*see Anxiety*)

PHOTOPHOBIA

(*see also Eyestrain*)

Photophobia is unusual intolerance of light. It occurs in conditions such as measles, rubella, meningitis and inflammation of the eyes.

Exercises

Neck warm-ups. Pose of Tranquillity (*page 51*), The Crocodile (*page 52*), Pose of a Child (*page 55*), Palming (*page 71*). Eye Exercises, Eye Splashing, Nasal Wash.

Nutrients

Vitamin A, the B vitamins (particularly B_2, inositol), vitamins C, E, zinc.

PID (PELVIC INFLAMMATORY DISEASE)

(*see also Menstrual Irregularities and Pain*)

PID is ascending infection from the vagina or cervix to the uterus and its attachments – particularly the fallopian tubes. Symptoms include: purulent vaginal discharge, abdominal pain, fever, chills, nausea, vomiting and general weakness.

Almost any bacterium (germ) can cause PID, but the most frequent agents are *Neisseria gonorrhoea* and *Chlamydia trachomatis*. PID may also result from the insertion of an intra-uterine contraceptive device, from an abortion or from sexual intercourse with a man who has a sexually transmitted disease.

Exercises

The following exercises, practised regularly, are useful for maintaining pelvic and general health: The Butterfly (*page 34*), Squatting Posture (*page 39*), Knee and Thigh Stretch (*page 39*), Mountain Posture (*page 40*), Chest Expander (*page 47*), Supine Knee Squeeze (*page 49*), Pose of Tranquillity (*page 51*), The Crocodile (*page 52*), Star Posture (*page 53*), Spread Leg Stretch (*page 54*), Pose of a Child (*page 55*), Pelvic Stretch (*page 56*), The Camel (*page 56*), Lying Twist (*page 35*), Side Leg raise (*page 59*), Spinal Twist (*page 61*), Cat Stretch series (*pages 69–70*). Alternate Nostril Breathing (*page 73*). Anti-Anxiety Breath, Breathing Away Pain (for pain relief), Cleansing Breath (Simple), Complete Breath, Humming Breath. Meditation. Perineal Exercise and Sitz Bath.

Nutrients

Vitamin A, the B vitamins (particularly B_2, B_3, B_5, B_6, B_9, B_{12}), vitamins C, E, EFAs (omega-6 fatty acids), zinc.

PILES

(*see Haemorrhoids*)

PMS

(*see Menstrual Irregularities*)

PROSTATE GLAND DISORDERS

The prostate gland encircles the neck of the bladder and urethra in the male. The gland secretes a thin, opalescent, slightly alkaline fluid that forms part of semen.

Enlargement of the prostate gland is common, especially after middle age. This causes troublesome symptoms such as the need to urinate frequently (often at night), an inability to completely empty the bladder, and difficulty or pain in urinating.

Cancer of the prostate is the second most common cancer in men, especially after 50 years of age. The cause is unknown, but sex hormones and viruses may play a part. After its symptomless early stages, cancer of the prostate produces the same symptoms as an enlarged prostate, when the growing tumour restricts the normal flow of urine. There may also be blood in the urine.

Exercises

Practise as many of the following as regularly as you can to help maintain a healthy prostate gland. The Butterfly (*page 34*), Squatting posture (*page 39*), Knee and Thigh Stretch (*page 39*), Rock-and-Roll (*page 36*), Stick Posture (*page 48*), Supine Knee Squeeze (*page 49*), Pose of Tranquillity (*page 51*), The Crocodile (*page 52*), Spread Leg Stretch (*page 54*), Pelvic Stretch (*page 56*), The Camel (*page 56*), Half Locust (*page 58*), Lying Twist (*page 35*), Side Leg Raise (*page 59*), Angle posture (*page 61*), Spinal Twist (*page 61*), Half Shoulderstand (*page 62*), Full Shoulderstand (*page 63*), Sun Salutations (*pages 65–68*), Alternate Nostril Breathing

127

(*page 73*). Anti-Anxiety Breath, Breathing Away Pain (for pain relief), Cleansing Breath (Simple), Complete Breath. Meditation.

Nutrients

Vitamins A, C, E, EFAs (omega-6 fatty acids), zinc, dietary fibre.

PRURITUS

(*see Itching*)

PSORIASIS

(*see Skin Problems*)

RAYNAUD'S DISEASE

(*see also Arthritis*)

Raynaud's Disease is a spastic disorder of the small arteries of the fingers and sometimes toes, which impairs blood flow. Occurring most often in women between 18 and 30 years of age, it is characterized by an abnormal constriction of the blood vessels of the extremities upon exposure to cold or to emotional stress.

Symptoms include intermittent attacks of pallor or blueness (cyanosis) of the digits (usually the fingers), numbness and feeling cold. This condition is sometimes associated with the development of rheumatoid arthritis, and may also be a reaction to certain chemicals or drugs.

Treatment includes: keeping the extremities warm with woollen gloves and socks; taking good care of the hands; avoiding contact with cold materials; avoiding tobacco use and learning to relax.

Exercises

Warm-ups for the hands and shoulders. The Butterfly (*page 34*), Mountain Posture (*page 40*), Cow Head Posture (*page 41*), The Flower (*page 42*), Chest Expander (*page 47*), Rock-and-Roll (*page 36*), Pose of Tranquillity (*page 51*), The Crocodile (*page 52*), Sun Salutations (*pages 65–68*), Candle Concentration (*page 71*). Alternate Nostril Breathing (*page 73*). Cleansing Breath (Dynamic), Complete Breath, Humming Breath. Meditation.

Nutrients

Vitamin A, the B vitamins (particularly B_3, B_5, B_6, choline, inositol), vitamin C, flavonoids, vitamin E, EFAs, calcium, magnesium, lecithin.

REPRODUCTIVE PROBLEMS

Reproductive problems often have a marked psychological component. For example, fear, guilt or resentment related to genital functions can generate sexual difficulties in both sexes. In women, stress, subconscious needs and suppressed emotions can all produce menstrual problems.

Obtaining help in identifying underlying causes of reproductive problems is an excellent first step towards overcoming these ailments.

Yoga trains you to develop an awareness of your inner needs, and equips you to deal with them constructively. It can assist you to overcome physical obstacles that interfere with good health, and provide the body with reinforcement for healing itself. The many breathing, relaxation and meditation techniques are also excellent tools for helping you deal effectively with stress.

Exercises

The Butterfly (*page 34*), Squatting posture (*page 39*), Knee and Thigh Stretch (*page 39*), Mountain Posture (*page 40*), Angle Balance (*page 42*), Abdominal Lift (*page 47*), Fish Posture (*page 49*), Pose of Tranquillity (*page 51*), The Crocodile (*page 52*), Star Posture (*page 53*), Spread Leg Stretch (*page 54*), Pose of a Child (*page 55*), Pelvic Stretch (*page 56*), The Camel (*page 56*), The Cobra (*page 57*), Half Locust (*page 58*), The Bow (*page 58*), Side Leg Raise (*page 59*), Spinal Twist (*page 61*), Half Shoulderstand (*page 62*), Full Shoulderstand (*page 63*). Alternate Nostril Breathing (*page 73*). Anti-Anxiety Breath, Cleansing Breath (Dynamic), Complete Breath. Meditation. Perineal Exercise.

Nutrients

Vitamin A, the B vitamins (particularly B_2, B_3, B_6), anti-stress factors, vitamins C, E, EFAs, calcium, chromium, iron, magnesium, manganese, molybdenum, selenium, zinc, carnitine.

RHEUMATISM

(*see Arthritis*)

RHEUMATOID ARTHRITIS

(*see Arthritis*)

SCOLIOSIS

(*see Backache*)

SEASICKNESS

(*see Nausea*)

SEBORRHOEA

(*see Alopecia*)

SEIZURES

(*see Epilepsy*)

SEXUAL PROBLEMS

(*see Reproductive Problems*)

SHIN SPLINTS

Shin splints is a name given to the pain and sensitivity to touch in the front part of the lower legs that can follow strenuous overexercise. The discomfort results from diminished blood supply to the muscles and minute tears and inflammation of the muscles and connective tissue.

Exercises

Leg warm-ups. Squatting Posture (*page 39*) (alternate with rising onto your toes), Knee and Thigh Stretch (*page 39*), The Tree (*page 44*), Balance Posture (*page 45*), Eagle posture (*page 46*), Rock-and-Roll (*page 36*), Pose of Tranquillity (*page 51*), Spread Leg Stretch (*page 53*), The Plough (*page 54*), Pelvic Stretch (*page 56*), Sun Salutations (*pages 65–68*). Alternate Nostril Breathing (*page 73*). Breathing Away Pain (for pain relief), Cleansing Breath (Dynamic), Complete Breath.

Nutrients

Vitamin A, the B vitamins (particularly B_1, B_2, B_3, B_5, B_6, B_9, B_{12}, biotin) anti-stress factors, vitamins C, D, E, EFAs (omega-6 fatty acids), calcium, copper, magnesium, potassium, selenium, sodium, zinc.

SINUSITIS

(see also Nasal Allergy)

The inflammation of a sinus – especially one which opens into the nasal cavity – can be caused by allergy, bacteria or viruses; also be inadequate drainage because of polyps, chronic inflammation of the nasal lining or general debility.

Exercises

(see Nasal Allergy)

Nutrients

(see Nasal Allergy)

SKIN PROBLEMS

(see also Allergies and Itching)

Some skin problems respond well to simple treatments and minor changes in diet. Others require medications and therapies best given or recommended by a medical doctor or skin specialist (dermatologist).

Acne – for information, see the specific entry.

Abnormal dryness may occur as a result of a thyroid gland disorder or diabetes.

Eczema (dermatitis) generally refers to inflammation of the skin. It largely results from an irritant such as a chemical or cosmetic, but can also be triggered by too much heat, sweating, substances producing allergy (allergens), infection and emotional stress. (Emotional stress is possibly the most potent trigger factor).

Psoriasis is a chronic, recurring, non-contagious condition which is thought to be inherited. The course of this disorder is affected by injury, infection, stress and drugs.

Rash is a word generally applied to any 'breaking out' of the skin, especially in connection with contagious diseases. It is one of the most common side effects of a number of medications.

Wrinkling of the skin, if permanent, may be the result of ageing. If temporary, it can be due to prolonged immersion in water or dehydration.

For more information on the skin and various aspects of skin care, please refer to my book entitled *Super Healthy Hair, Skin and Nail* (*see the Bibliography for details*).

Exercises

(see Acne)

Nutrients

(see Acne)

SLE (SYSTEMIC LUPUS ERYTHEMATOSUS)

(see Immune System Disorders)

SORE THROAT

(see Colds)

SLEEPLESSNESS

(*see Insomnia*)

SMOKING

(*see Addiction*)

STOMACH DISORDERS

(*see also Flatulence*)

Acid stomach is the return of digestive acid into the mouth, or excessive production of stomach acid. There is often a burning sensation (heartburn) in the 'food-pipe' (oesophagus) as well as belching.

Dyspepsia (indigestion) refers to imperfect or painful digestion. Usually symptomatic of other disorders, it is characterized by vague abdominal discomfort, belching, heartburn, loss of appetite, weight loss, nausea or vomiting. Symptoms increase in times of stress.

Digestive system diseases that cause indigestion include peptic ulcers, gall bladder disease and hiatus (diaphragmatic) hernia.

Gastric ulcer – for information, see *Ulcers, page 134.*

Gastritis is inflammation of the stomach, characterized by pain or tenderness in the area of the stomach as well as by nausea and vomiting.

The causes are generally unknown, but the condition may result from infection, excessive alcohol intake and dietary indiscretions, or it can be because of an excess or deficiency of stomach acid.

Peptic ulcer – for information, see *Ulcers, page 134.*

Exercises

Japanese Sitting Position (*page 38*), Mountain Posture (*page 40*), Angle balance (*page 42*), The Tree (*page 44*), Chest Expander (*page 47*), Stick Posture (*page 48*), Pose of Tranquillity (*page 51*), The Crocodile (*page 52*), Candle Concentration (*page 71*). Alternate Nostril Breathing (*page 73*). Anti-Anxiety Breath, Cleansing Breath (Simple), Complete Breath, Humming Breath. Meditation.

Nutrients

Vitamin A, the B vitamins (particularly B_1, B_2, B_3, B_5, B_6, B_9, choline, PABA), anti-stress factors, vitamins C, E, K, calcium, magnesium, manganese, potassium.

STRESS

(*see also Anxiety, Insomnia and Panic Attack*)

Stress is the non-specific response by the body to any demand made upon it. It becomes a problem when demands tax or exceed our adaptive resources.

When people are under stress various changes take place in the body. These include: increased muscle tension (such as tight jaws and rigid back muscles); faster pulse rate; elevated blood pressure; faster rate of breathing; impairment of digestion; shortened blood clotting time; withdrawal of minerals from bones; mobilization of fats from storage deposits and retention of an abnormal amount of salt.

Any event, circumstance or other agent causing or leading to stress is called a stressor. Stressors include fear, guilt, regret, frustration and uncertainty. They can have a great impact on the immune system and seriously undermine health.

The key to managing stress effectively is to maintain a high standard of health. Inherent in this is the daily practice of some form of relaxation.

Exercises

Mountain Posture (*page 40*), The Tree (*page 44*), Chest Expander (*page 47*), Rock-and-Roll (*page 36*), Pose of Tranquillity (*page 51*), The Crocodile (*page 52*), Back-stretching Posture (*page 53*), The Plough (*page 54*), Pose of a Child (*page 55*), The Cobra (*page 57*), Half Moon (*page 60*), Spinal Twist (*page 61*), Half Shoulderstand (*page 62*), Full Shoulderstand (*page 63*), Sun Salutations (*pages 65–68*). Alternate Nostril Breathing (*page 73*). Anti-Anxiety Breath, Cleansing Breath (Dynamic), Complete Breath, Sighing Breath, Humming Breath. Meditation.

Nutrients

Vitamin A, the B vitamins (particularly B_2, B_3, B_5, B_6, choline), anti-stress factors, vitamin C, flavonoids, vitamins D, E, EFAs, calcium, magnesium, manganese, potassium, silicon.

STRESS-RELATED INCONTINENCE

(*see Incontinence (of urine)*)

SWELLING

(*see Oedema*)

TEETH, GRINDING OF

(*see Bruxism*)

TENDINITIS

Tendinitis is inflammation of a tendon – the fibrous tissue connecting muscles to bones.

A good preventive measure is the regular performance of appropriate exercises to strengthen the joints supporting the tissues.

Exercises

Warm-ups. Cow Head Posture (*page 40*), Eagle Posture (*page 46*), Chest Expander (*page 54*), Spinal Twist (*page 61*), Sun Salutations (*pages 65–68*). Alternate Nostril Breathing (*page 73*). Anti-Anxiety Breath, Breathing Away Pain (for pain relief), Cleansing Breath (Simple and Dynamic), Complete Breath.

Nutrients

Vitamin A, the B vitamins (particularly B_1, B_2, B_3, B_5, B_6, B_9, biotin), anti-stress factors, vitamin C, flavonoids, vitamins D, E, EFAs, calcium, magnesium, silicon,

TENSION

(*see Stress*)

THYROID GLAND PROBLEMS

The thyroid gland is a gland of internal secretion, located in the base of the neck. It secretes the hormone thyroxine.

Goitre is an enlargement of the thyroid gland. It may occur because of a lack of iodine in the diet, inflammation from infection or either an under- or over-functioning of the gland.

Hypothyroidism is caused by a deficiency of the thyroid secretion, and results in lowered basal metabolism. Symptoms may include dry skin and hair, obesity, slow pulse, low blood pressure and sluggishness of all functions.

Thyrotoxicosis is a toxic condition resulting from overactivity of the thyroid gland. Symptoms include: rapid heart action, tremors, enlargement of the gland, abnormal protrusion of the eyeballs, nervous symptoms and weight loss.

Exercises

Pose of Tranquillity (*page 51*), Pose of a Child (*page 55*), Spinal Twist (*page 61*), Half Shoulderstand (*page 62*), Full Shoulderstand (*page 63*), Mock Headstand (*page 64*), Sun Salutations (*pages 65–68*). Alternate Nostril Breathing (*page 73*). Anti-Anxiety Breath, Cleansing Breath (Dynamic), Complete Breath. Meditation.

Nutrients

Vitamin A, carotenes, the B vitamins (particularly B_2, B_5, B_6, choline), anti-stress factors, vitamins C, E, EFAs, chromium, iodine, manganese, selenium, zinc, dietary fibre.

TMJ (TEMPOROMANDIBULAR JOINT) SYNDROME

(*see also Bruxism, Pain and Stress*)

TMJ syndrome refers to pain and inflammation in the jaw joints (temporo-mandibular) and adjoining muscles. The pain worsens with chewing, and clicking sounds can be heard. There may also be ringing in the ears (tinnitus).

One cause of TMJ syndrome is grinding the teeth and contracting the jaw muscles in an unconscious attempt to relieve muscle tension generated by stress. Other causes include ill-fitting dentures or an attempt to compensate for a faulty alignment ('bite') between the upper and lower jaws.

The condition is more common in women than in men, and the risk of TMJ syndrome increases with osteoarthritis and stress. Preventive measures include refraining from grinding the teeth, and the regular practice of tension-relieving exercises.

Exercises

The Lion (*page 43*), following neck and shoulder warm-ups. Be aware of tension accumulating in your jaws; unclench your teeth. Practice the Pose of Tranquillity (*page 51*) daily, as well as breathing exercises: Anti-Anxiety Breath, Cleansing Breath (Simple), Complete Breath, Humming Breath, Sighing Breath. Meditation.

Nutrients

The B vitamins (particularly B_5), anti-stress factors, calcium, magnesium.

TOBACCO DEPENDENCE

(*see Addiction*)

TRAVEL SICKNESS

(*see Nausea*)

ULCERATIVE COLITIS

(*see Inflammatory Bowel Disease*)

ULCERS (DUODENAL, GASTRIC, PEPTIC)

A *gastric ulcer* is an ulcer of the mucous membrane lining of the stomach. A *duodenal ulcer* is an ulcer of the first part of the small intestine (duodenum). Both are caused by the action of acidic stomach (gastric) secretions.

The term *peptic ulcer* refers to ulceration of either the stomach or the duodenum.

Stress ulcer refers to a peptic ulcer caused by acute or chronic stress, and is seen following some surgical procedures and in conditions that include brain trauma, burns, acute infection, prolonged treatment with steroids and central nervous system diseases.

Exercises

Mountain Posture (*page 40*), The Tree (*page 44*), Chest Expander (*page 47*), Stick Posture (*page 48*), Pose of Tranquillity (*page 51*), The Crocodile (*page 52*), Pose of a Child (*page 55*), Sun Salutations (*pages 65–68*). Candle Concentration (*page 71*). Alternate Nostril Breathing (*page 73*). Anti-Anxiety Breath, Humming Breath. Meditation.

Nutrients

Vitamin A, the B vitamins (particularly B_6), anti-stress factors, vitamins E, K, EFAs, iron (if anaemia occurs, or if there is a tendency thereto).

URINARY PROBLEMS

(*see Cystitis, Incontinence of Urine and Prostate Gland Disorders*)

URTICARIA (HIVES, NETTLE RASH)

(*see Allergies, Itching and Skin Problems*)

VARICOSE VEINS

Enlarged, twisted, superficial veins that may occur in almost any part of the body but are mostly seen in the legs. The main cause for them is incompetent valves of the veins, which may have been present at birth or acquired.

The development of varicose veins is promoted and aggravated by pregnancy, obesity and occupations requiring prolonged standing.

Preventive measures include: avoiding anything that impedes the return of blood in the veins (such as the wearing of garters and tight girdles), crossing the legs at the knees, prolonged sitting, prolonged standing and being overweight.

Remember to *check with your doctor* for permission to do the exercises in this book.

Exercises

See general cautions (Chapter 4). Legs Up (*page 50*), Pose of Tranquillity (*page 51*), Half Shoulderstand (*page 62*), Full Shoulderstand (*page 63*). Alternate Nostril Breathing (*page 73*). Complete Breath, Cleansing Breath (Simple), Humming Breath.

Nutrients

Vitamin A, the B vitamins (particularly B_6), vitamin C, flavonoids, vitamin E, EFAs, calcium, copper, magnesium, zinc, dietary fibre, lecithin.

VERTIGO

(*see Dizziness*)

VISION PROBLEMS

(*see Eyestrain and Photophobia*)

VOMITING

(*see Nausea*)

WEAKNESS

(*see Fatigue and ME*)

WEIGHT PROBLEMS

(*see Anorexia and Obesity*)

WIND (GAS)

(*see Flatulence*)

WRINKLES

(*see Skin Problems*)

BIBLIOGRAPHY

Airola, Paavo. PhD, ND. *How to Get Well*, Phoenix, Arizona: Health Plus, 1974

A'nanda, M'arga. *Teaching Asanas*, Los Altos Hills, California: Amrit Publications, 1973

Anderson, Kenneth. *Symptoms After 40*, New York: Stonesong Press, 1987

Benson, Herbert. *The Relaxation Response*, New York: William Morrow, 1975

Blake, Leslie Stevenson. RN, BSN. 'Sick and Tired', *The Canadian Nurse*, vol. 89, no. 7, August (1993), pp. 25–32.

Brena, Steven F., MD. *Yoga & Medicine*, Baltimore, Maryland: Penguin Books, 1973

Bricklin, Mark. *The Practical Encyclopaedia of Natural Healing* (revised edition), Emmaus, Pennsylvania: Rodale Press, 1983

Brown, Barbara B. *Stress and the Art of Biofeedback*, New York: Harper & Row, 1977

Corbin, Charles B. and Lindsey, Ruth. *Concepts of Physical Fitness with Laboratories* (7th edn), Dubuque, Iowa: Wm. C. Brown, 1991

Cousins, Norman. *Head First. The Biology of Hope*, New York: E.P. Dutton, 1989

Davis, Adelle. *Let's Get Well*, London: Thorsons, 1972

Let's Eat Right to Keep Fit, London: Thorsons, 1970

Dunne, Lavon J. *Nutrition Almanac* (3rd edn), New York: McGraw-Hill, 1990

Faelton, Sharon, and the Editors of 'Prevention Magazine'. *The Complete Book of Minerals for Health*. Emmaus, Pennsylvania: Rodale Press, 1981

Feinstein, Alice (Ed.). *The Visual Encyclopaedia of Natural Healing*, Emmaus, Pennsylvania: Rodale Press, 1991

Gardner, A. Ward. MD. *Good Housekeeping Dictionary of Symptoms*, New York: Good Housekeeping Books, 1976

Gelb, Harold, DMD, and Siegel, Paula M. *Killing Pain Without Prescription*, London: Thorsons, 1983

Gomez, Dr Joan. *A Dictionary of Symptoms*, New York: Stein and Day, 1985

Graham, Judy, and Odent, Dr Michael. *The Z Factor. How Zinc is Vital to Your Health*, London: Thorsons, 1986.

Girffith, H. Winter, M.D. *Complete Guide to Symptoms, Illness & Surgery*, New York: The Body Press/Perigee Books, 1989

Hendler, Sheldon Saul, MD, PhD. *The Doctors' Vitamin and Mineral Encyclopaedia*, New York: Simon and Schuster, 1990

Hewitt, James. *The Complete Book of Yoga*, New York: Schocken Books, 1977

Humphrey, Dennis, EdD. 'Flexibility for the Middle and Low Back', *The Physician and Sports Medicine*, vol. 17, no. 10, October (1989)

Iyengar, B.K.S. *Light on Yoga*, London: Thorsons, 1966

Iyengar, Geeta S. *Yoga: A Gem for Women*, Palo Alto, California: Timeless Books, 1990

Kaufmann, Klaus. *Silica. The Forgotten Nutrient*, Burnaby, Canada: Alive Books, 1990

Kuvalayananda, Swami, and Vinekar, Dr. S. L. *Yogic Therapy*, New Delhi: Central Health Education Bureau, Ministry of Health, 1971

Mayes, Adrienne, BSc, PhD. *The Dictionary of Nutritional Health*, London: Thorsons, 1986.

Mills, Simon, MA, and Finando, Steven J., PhD. *Alternatives in Healing*, New York: New American Library, 1988.

Mindell, Earl. *Earl Mindell's Vitamin Bible*, New York: Warner Books, 1979

Monro, Dr Robin, Nagarathna, Dr R., and Nagendra, Dr H. R. *Yoga for Common Ailments*, London: Gaia Books, 1990

Moyers, Bill. *Healing and the Mind*, New York: Doubleday, 1993

Murray, Michael, ND, and Pizzorno, Joseph, ND. *Encyclopaedia of Natural Medicine*, Rocklin, California: Prima Publishing, 1991

Noble, Elizabeth, RPT. *Essential Exercises for the Childbearing Year*, Boston: Houghton Mifflin, 1976

Pelletier, Kenneth R., PhD. *Mind as Healer, Mind as Slayer*, New York: Delacorte Press, 1977

Peterson, Vicki. *The Natural Food Catalog*, New York; Arco Publishing, 1978

'Prevention Magazine', Editors of *The Healing Foods*. Emmaus, Pennsylvania: Rodale Press, 1991

Quillin, Patrick, PhD, RD. *Healing Nutrients*, Chicago: Contemporary Books, 1987

Rama, Swani, Ballentine, Rudolph, MD, and Hymes, Alan, MD. *Science of Breath. A Practical Guide*, Honesdale, Pennsylvania: The Himalayan International Institute of Yoga Science and Philosophy, 1979

Rogers, Jean (Ed.). *The Healing Foods Cookbook*, Emmaus, Pennsylvania: Rodale Press, 1991

Rona, Zoltan P., MD, MSc. *The Joy of Health. A doctor's guide to nutrition and alternative medicine*, Willowdale, Ontario: Hounslow Press, 1991

Rosenfeld, Isadore, MD. *Symptoms*, New York: Simon and Schuster, 1989

Saltman, Paul, PhD, Gurin, Joel, and Mothner, Ira. *The University of California San Diego Nutrition Book*, Boston: Little, Brown and Company, 1993

Saraswati, Swami Satyananda. *Asana Pranayama Mudra Bandha*, Bihar, India: Bihar School of Yoga, 1977

Satchidananda, Yogiraj Sri Swami. *Integral Yoga Hatha*, New York: Henry Holt and Company, 1970

Schatz, Mary Pullig, MD. *Back Care Basics. A Doctor's Gentle Yoga Program for Back and Neck Pain Relief*, Berkeley, California: Rodmell Press, 1992

Schroeder, Steven A., et al. (Eds.) *Current Medical Diagnosis & Treatment*, East Norwalk, Connecticut: Appleton & Lange, 1990

Sharma, Pandit Shiv. *Yoga Against Spinal Pain*, London; George G. Harrap, 1971

Shreeve, Dr Caroline M. *The Alternative Dictionary of Symptoms and Cures*, London: Century Hutchinson, 1986

Simon, Harvey B. *Staying Well. Your Complete Guide to Disease Prevention*, Boston: Houghton Mifflin, 1992

Smolan, Rick, Moffitt, Phillip, and Naythons, Matthew, MD. *The Power to Heal. Ancient Arts & Modern Medicine*, New York: Prentice Hall Press, 1990

Stanton, Rosemary. *Eating for Peak Performance*, Sydney: Allen & Unwin, 1988

Stanway, Dr Andrew. *Alternative Medicine. A Guide to Natural Therapies*, Harmondsworth: Penguin Books, 1986

Stearn, Jess. *Yoga, Youth and Reincarnation*, New York: Doubleday, 1965

Thomas, Clayon L., MD. MPH (Ed.). *Taber's Cylopedic Medical Dictionary*, (16th edn), Philadelphia: F.A. Davis, 1985

Van Lysbeth, André. *Yoga Self-Taught*, New York: Barnes & Noble, 1973

Van Straten, Michael, ND, DO. *The Complete Natural Health Consultant*, New York: Prentice Hall Press, 1987.

Vishnudevananda, Swami. *The Complete Illustrated Book of Yoga*, New York; Harmony Books, 1988

Weil, andrew, MD. *Natural Health, Natural Medicine. A Comprehensive Manual for Wellness and Self-Care*, Boston: Houghton Mifflin, 1990

Weller, Stella. *Pain-Free Periods*, London: Thorsons, 1993

The Yoga Back Book. London: Thorsons, 1993

Easy Pregnancy with Yoga, London: Thorsons, 1991

Super Healthy Hair, Skin & Nails, London: Thorsons, 1991

Santé Immunitaire Naturelle, Geneva: Éditions Jouvence, 1991

Werbach, Melvyn, MD. *Healing Through Nutrition*, New York: HarperCollins*Publishers*, 1993

Yesudian, Selvarajan, and Haich, Elisabeth. *Yoga and Health*, London: Unwin Paperbacks, 1987

Yogendra, Smt. Sitadevi. *Yoga Simplified for Women*, Santa Cruz, Bombay: The Yoga Institute, 1972

Yudkin, John. *The Penguin Encyclopaedia of Nutrition*, New York: Viking 1985.

INDEX